GOD'S WORD
FOR A JR. HIGH WORLD

Teachings of Jesus

Gospel Light

Tim Baker, Author
Kara Eckmann Powell, General Editor

Gospel Light is an evangelical Christian publisher dedicated to serving the local church. We believe God's vision for Gospel Light is to provide church leaders with biblical, user-friendly materials that will help them evangelize, disciple and minister to children, youth and families.

We hope this Gospel Light resource will help you discover biblical truth for your own life and help you minister to youth. God bless you in your work.

For a free catalog of resources from Gospel Light please contact your Christian supplier or contact us at 1-800-4-GOSPEL.

PUBLISHING STAFF
William T. Greig, Publisher
Dr. Elmer L. Towns, Senior Consulting Publisher
Dr. Gary S. Greig, Senior Consulting Editor
Jill Honodel, Managing Editor
Pam Weston, Editor
Patti Pennington Virtue, Assistant Editor
Christi Goeser, Editorial Assistant
Kyle Duncan, Associate Publisher
Bayard Taylor, M.Div., Senior Editor, Theological and Biblical Issues
Kevin Parks, Cover Designer
Debi Thayer, Designer
Natalie Chenault and Miles McPherson, Contributing Writers

You may make copies of portions of this book with a clean conscience if:

- you (or someone in your organization) are the original purchaser;
- you are using the copies you make for a noncommercial purpose (such as teaching or promoting your ministry) within your church or organization;
- you follow the instructions provided in this book.

However, it is ILLEGAL for you to make copies if:

- you are using the material to promote, advertise or sell a product or service other than for ministry fund-raising;
- you are using the material in or on a product for sale;
- you or your organization are **not** the original purchaser of this book.

By following these guidelines you help us keep our products affordable.

Thank you,

Gospel Light

As a professor and trainer of youth ministers, this is the best concept for junior high discipleship that I have ever seen. I love this curriculum not only because it gets Scripture into the hands and hearts of junior highers, but it does it in a way that they can grab hold of and enjoy. There is none better than Kara Eckmann Powell to ensure the integrity, depth and appropriateness of this tool. The **Pulse** curriculum is going to be a landmark resource for years to come. —**Chapman R. Clark, Ph.D.**, Associate Professor of Youth and Family Ministry, Fuller Theological Seminary

What I really appreciate about the **Pulse** series is that it fleshes out what I consider to be two absolute essentials for great curriculum: biblical depth and active learning. It is obvious that this is a curriculum designed by youth workers who care about junior high kids and who deeply care about helping them grow in their walk with Jesus. —**Duffy Robbins**, Associate Professor, Department of Youth Ministry, Eastern College

The youth leader's biggest challenge today is to relevantly translate the gospel to this generation. Kara has written a game plan for doing just that! **Pulse** is a curriculum that will help God's Word to become real for your students and will help you to reach a diverse generation—from the edgy/techno savvy to the more conservative student. It will produce a life change in (you)th! —**Larry Acosta**, President, The Hispanic Ministry Center

Pulse will help youth leaders create a great learning environment, provide a solid biblical education and challenge students to practice their faith daily. If leaders will use the variety of learning activities and creative teaching ideas, they will bring excellence to every lesson while enjoying the benefit of a simplified preparation time. —**Lynn Ziegenfuss**, Vice President of People Development, Youth for Christ/USA

In a world where Truth has been hidden in tolerance and where God has become the god of one's choice, Truth and solid biblical principles must be imparted to our students. **Pulse** CAPITALIZES both God and Truth. It's real, it's relevant, and it's *the* Truth! —**Monty L. Hipp**, Youth Communicator, Creative Communications

This is the best junior high/middle school curriculum to come out in years. Students will love this curriculum. —**Jim Burns, Ph.D.**, President, National Institute of Youth Ministry

Wow! I'm impressed with the quality and the message this curriculum brings to millennials. It's going to be fun to use this material with kids! —**Charles Kim**, *JDM—Journey Devotional Magazine*, The Oriental Mission Church

Kara knows students, teaching, youth workers and the Bible; and she mixes that with a passion for God's Word. It seems that everything Kara touches is gold and I believe this **Pulse** curriculum not only bears her name, but her touch as well. Thanks, Kara, for another great contribution to youth ministry. —**Doug Fields**, Youth Pastor, Saddleback Church, author, *Purpose Driven Youth Ministry*

Teachings of Jesus

CONTENTSCONTENTSCONTENTSCONTENTSCONTENTS

Unit I: Vertical: Our Relationship with God

Unit II: Horizontal: Our Relationship with Others

Dedication

For Fred Fitch, who introduced me to Jesus, Tim Schutz, who discipled me, and Chris Akers, who mentored me in youth ministry—without your influence in my life, this book could not have been written.

And for Jacqui: I'm so glad that I get to spend this life with you. Your wisdom, beauty and inspiration are out of this world. Thanks for letting me stay up late to write this book. I love you.

....You've Made the Right Choice in Choosing Pulse for Your Junior Highers

The Top Ten Reasons...

10. Junior highers equate who God is with what church is like. To them a boring youth ministry means a boring God.

Fun and variety are the twin threads that weave their way through this curriculum's every page.

9. Junior highers need and deserve youth workers who are expert trainers and teachers of biblical truth.

Every book is pulsating with youth leader tips and a full-length youth worker article designed to infuse YOU with more passion and skill for your ministry to junior highers.

8. Junior highers need ongoing reminders of the big idea of each session.

Wouldn't it be great if you could give your students devotionals every week to reinforce the learning goals of the session? Get this: YOU CAN because THIS CURRICULUM DOES.

7. Some of our world's most effective evangelists are junior highers.

Every session, and we mean EVERY session, concludes with an evangelism option that ties "the big idea" of the session to the big need to share Christ with others.

6. Since no two junior highers (or their leaders) look, think or act alike, no two junior high ministries look, think or act alike.

   Each step comes with three options that you can cut and paste to create a session that works best for YOUR students and YOUR personality.

5. Junior highers' growing minds are ready for more than just fun and games with a little Scripture thrown in.

   Scripture is the very skeleton of each session, giving it its shape, its form and its very life.

4. Junior highers learn best when they can see, taste, feel and experience the session.

   This curriculum involves students in every step through active learning and games to prove to students that following Christ is the greatest adventure ever.

3. Tragically, most junior highers are under challenged in their walks with Christ.

   We've packed the final step of each session with three options that serve to move students a few steps forward in their walks with Christ.

2. Junior highers tend to understand the Bible in bits and pieces and miss the big picture of all that God has done for them.

   This curriculum follows a strategic three-year plan that walks junior highers through the Bible, stopping at the most important points along the way.

1. Junior highers are moving through all sorts of changes—from getting a new body to getting a new locker.

   We've designed a curriculum that revolves around one simple vision: moving God's Word into a junior high world.

Moving Through Pulse

Since **Pulse** is vibrating with so many different learning activities, this guide will help you pick and choose the best possible options for *your* students.

THE SESSIONS

The six sessions are split into two stand-alone units, so you can choose to teach either three or six sessions at a time. Each session is geared to be 45 to 90 minutes long and is comprised of the following four steps.

IT'S YOUR MOVE

A training article for you, the youth worker, to show you *why* and *how* to see students' worlds changed by Christ to change the world.

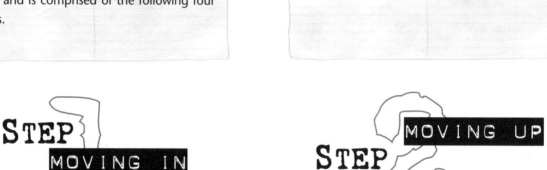

STEP 1 — MOVING IN

This first step helps students focus in on the theme of the lesson in a fun and engaging way through three options:

 MOVE IT—An active learning experience that may or may not involve all of your students.

 CHAT ROOM—Provocative, clear and simple questions to get your students thinking and chatting.

 FUN AND GAMES—Zany, creative and competitive games that may or may not involve all of your students.

STEP 2 — MOVING UP

The second step enables students to look up to God by relating the very words of Scripture to the session topic through three options:

 MOVE IT—An active learning experience that may or may not involve all of your students.

 CHAT ROOM—Provocative, clear and simple questions to get your students chatting about the Scripture lesson.

 PULSE POINTS—A message outline with simple points and meaningful illustrations to give students some massive truths about Scripture with hardly any preparation on your part.

STEP 3 — MOVING ON

STEP 4 — MOVING OUT

This step asks students to look inward and discover how God's Word connects with their own worlds through three options:

This final step leads students out into their world with specific challenges to apply at school, at home and with their friends through three options based on your students' growth potential:

 CHAT ROOM—Provocative, clear and simple questions to get your students chatting.

 LIGHT THE FIRE—For junior highers who may or may not be Christians and need easily accessible application ideas.

 REAL LIFE—A case study about someone (usually a junior higher) who needs your students' help figuring out what to do.

 FIRED UP—For students who are definitely Christians and are ready for more intense application ideas.

 TOUGH QUESTIONS—Four to six mind-stretching questions that challenge students to a new level of depth and integration.

 SPREAD THE FIRE—A special evangelism application idea for students with a passion to see others come to know Christ.

OTHER IMPORTANT MOVING PARTS

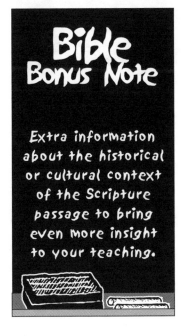

Bible Bonus Note

Extra information about the historical or cultural context of the Scripture passage to bring even more insight to your teaching.

Youth Leader Tip

Suggestions, options and/or other useful information to make your life easier or at least more interesting!

Devotions in Motion

WEEK FIVE: GRACE

Four devotionals for each session to keep the big idea moving through your junior highers' lives all week long.

ON THE MOVE—An appealing, easy-to-read handout you can give your junior highers to make sure they learn how to understand the Bible better.

The Stories and Parables of Jesus

In your hand you're holding an entire book devoted to helping you and your junior highers grow in and grasp the stories of Christ. Because most of Jesus' stories were parables, we decided to focus this book on parables, too (we figured if Jesus did it, why shouldn't we?).

We asked Miles McPherson, a national youth communicator and director of Miles Ahead Ministries, to answer a few simple questions geared to help you maximize the impact this series will have on your students.

WHY Should We Teach Junior Highers About Jesus' Parables?

The main reason to teach junior highers the stories, especially the parables in this book, is because Jesus taught them.

More specifically, parables by their very definition give us three reasons to teach them to junior highers. First, parables are short and simple stories designed to communicate a spiritual truth or religious principle by illustrating truth through a comparison or example drawn from everyday experiences. Jesus taught with stories because they are often the easiest way to teach eternal truths. This is especially true when you're staring at a roomful of concrete-thinking 13-year-olds.

Second, parables are based on the experiences of the listeners. When Jesus taught almost 2,000 years ago, even the simplest and least educated of listeners could follow His stories because they understood the types of people, the circumstances and the decisions involved.

It's Your Move!

Finally, parables have one central point. Although many applications could be drawn from Jesus' stories, there was always one major point. This simplicity fits junior highers perfectly. Their growing minds can only grab onto one or two principles at a time—as you've no doubt experienced when you've tried to teach them more than that!

HOW Should We Teach Junior Highers About Jesus' Parables?

As you set out to teach the parables, it is vital that you do two things. First, study the true biblical meaning and depend entirely on God's Word itself. As we learn in Hebrews 4:12, "For the word of God is living and active. Sharper than any doubled-edged sword, it penetrates even to dividing soul and spirit, joints and marrow; it judges the thoughts and attitudes of the heart." Make sure you focus more on what the Bible teaches than on your own common sense.

Second, let the words sink deep into you. Since the parables are eternal truths that are taught through practical everyday stories, you as the teacher must experience these truths yourself. Live their meanings. Only then can you fully understand their lessons. Be a visual aid for your students—and a life-sized one at that!

Miles McPherson
Director of Miles Ahead Ministries
Nationally known youth communicator

Contributors

Miles McPherson wears many hats. He is president of Miles Ahead Ministries and Miles Ahead Crusades, associate pastor of Horizon Christian Fellowship in San Diego, a national speaker for many organizations including Campus Crusade for Christ and Youth for Christ, and author of several books including The Power of Believing in Your Child, The Five "I Wills" of Satan, One Kid at a Time, 21 JumpStart and My Campus, My Mission. Miles and his wife, Debra, live in San Diego with their three children, Kelly, Kimmie and Miles.

Natalie Chenault, author of the student devotionals, enjoys diet soda and pudding cups. She attends Eastern College and loves hanging out with junior highers. She hopes to appear on Jeopardy! one day.

SESSIONONESESSIONONESESSIONONESESSIONONE

The Big Idea

God wants to talk to us. The question is, Are we ready to listen to Him?

Session Aims

In this session you will guide students to:

- Identify obstacles that make them deaf to what God is trying to say to them;
- Feel comforted knowing that God is actively pursuing them and longs to speak to them;
- Act by choosing one way they can listen to God this week.

The Biggest Verse

"He who has ears, let him hear."
Matthew 13:9

Other Important Verses

Psalms 15:1-5; 119:97-104; Matthew 13:1-23

Listening to God: The Sower

STEP
MOVING IN

This step gets students thinking about the things that block their hearing.

Option 1  Move It

You'll need A tape recorder and blank cassette tape, a TV, a short but interesting newspaper article, paper, pens or pencils and an adult friend.

Ahead of time, find a newspaper story that you think students would find interesting. Then set the tape recorder in front of a TV and turn the TV's volume on extremely loud. Ask your friend to begin reading and recording the newspaper article. The result should be that the story is barely recognizable because of the television noise in the background.

As students arrive, greet them and explain that today you're starting a new series on the teachings of Jesus. Explain: **Hey, I need your help with something. A friend wanted me to hear this story on tape, but I can't understand it. I need you to listen and see if you can make out what my friend is saying.**

Have students gather in groups of four and give each group paper and pens or pencils. Play the tape for the entire class, then have groups write what they think they're hearing.

When the tape is over, have groups report on what they heard on the tape. When they've all shared, ask:

How important is it to be able to hear and understand people?

Should you only listen to people you feel are important, like maybe a teacher or a friend?

What keeps us from hearing what others are saying to us? Answers may include being busy, self-centered or distracted.

Move the discussion to a deeper level by asking:

What's the difference between listening to a friend and listening to God?

Why do you think it's important to listen to God?

Transition to the next step by explaining: **Today we'll be talking about some of the things that interfere with**

God's voice in our lives and some ways that we can hear God better.

Option 2  Chat Room

You'll need A small ball, a candy prize, paper and pens or pencils.

Greet students and explain that you're starting a new series on the teachings of Jesus, but first you want to do a quick activity together. Explain that you're going to ask a question, then throw the ball to a student. The person who gets the ball needs to answer the question, then throw it to another student, who will then answer the same question. This continues until everyone has answered the question or until you feel momentum is dying and it's time to introduce another question.

Suggested questions include: What is your middle name? What is the third digit in your phone number? What is the best after-school snack you've had this week? What is something you can share with us that probably no one else here knows?

After a few minutes, distribute papers and pens or pencils and ask each student to list as many people's answers as they can, such as "Jose's best after-school snack is eggplant." (Jose's got some unusual tastes, obviously.)

Give a candy prize to the student who can remember the most answers. Ask:

What made it tough to remember what people said?

When we're talking with our friends, why is it sometimes hard to listen to them? Answers can include that we're too busy, distracted and self-centered.

Why is it important to listen to the people you care about?

Transition to a deeper level by asking, **Why is it important to listen to God?**

Explain: **Listening is essential for developing a good friendship, whether it is our friendship with God or our friendships with our friends or family. For any friendship to grow stronger, we've got to be willing to listen.**

Option 3 Fun and Games

You'll need Several sheets of paper and pens or pencils.

Divide students into groups of six. Distribute paper and pens or pencils and instruct students to write messages that they might want to communicate to people. Some ideas include phrases like "Hey, I think you're cool!," "You have something caught in your teeth" or "I like that shirt you're wearing today." Allow two minutes for students to write as many statements as they can think of—a different statement on each sheet of paper. When time is up, ask: **Have you ever noticed that hearing and understanding what people say isn't always easy? Well, today you're going to have a really hard time hearing people.**

Have the small groups stand up and designate two students from each group as the "listeners." Instruct these students to stand at arm's length apart in a circle facing toward the middle of the circle. Assign two more students from each group the role of the "talkers." Have these students kneel in a tight circle in the middle of the listeners' circle, shoulder to shoulder, facing out toward the listeners. Give the talkers the papers with the statements written on them and instruct them to begin wadding the papers into tight paper balls. The remaining students are the "interferers" who will attempt to obstruct the communication between the talkers and the listeners.

The game works like this: The talkers will kneel in their circle and toss the paper wads at the listeners. The interferers will run around and try and keep the wads from the listeners. Once the listeners have caught a wad of paper, the interferers cannot rip it from their hands.

As a signal to get the game started, yell: **Let's get talking!** Give students 90 seconds to play; then have students switch roles and repeat the game.

Once you've calmed them down (with the adrenaline of junior highers it may take a few minutes), have them sit down; then discuss:

How is this game like the communication that we have with others? Sometimes things interfere with communication. Sometimes it's hard to hear our friends.

What are some things that can interfere with our communication with others? Answers can include getting too busy, self-centered or distracted by other things.

Transition to a deeper level of discussion by asking: **When have you had difficulty listening to God?** Explain to students that good communication, whether it be with God or others, is the result of both talking and listening. Today we're going to learn how we can listen to God better.

Youth Leader Tip

Anyone who has stood in front of a bunch of junior high students has felt like they were speaking Swahili to a roomful of Indonesian bakers. Let's face it, we don't always feel like we're communicating with our students. Remember these ideas to help you when you're feeling like you're completely out of touch:

Go Nuts. When you feel like you just aren't communicating, exaggerate everything you do. Shout directions. Make weird faces. Stand on your head. But remember, there's a fine line between being crazy and looking stupid. Find that line and live above it.

Hang On. Sometimes kids aren't following you, but they haven't totally given up yet. Remember, keep pressing on as you teach. If you find you need to stop a lesson, you can, but *only* if you're sure students have already checked out.

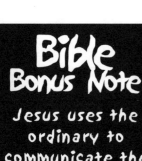

Bible Bonus Note

Jesus uses the ordinary to communicate the extraordinary things about God's kingdom here. When Jesus was speaking about the different types of soil, He was using something that would be familiar to almost all of His listeners.

• In Palestine there were two ways to sow seed. Both ways—tossing it on the ground or tying a sack of seeds on the back of a donkey—caused some seeds to land in places where it wouldn't grow.

• Farmers usually made their fields in long narrow strips, leaving room between

STEP 2 — MOVING UP

This step helps students realize that they need to be ready to listen to God all the time.

Option 1 — Move It

You'll need Several Bibles, transparent or masking tape, paper and pens or pencils.

Ahead of time, write the following four area descriptions and their corresponding Scripture passages each on a separate sheet of paper: The path, Matthew 13:3,4; The rocky soil, Matthew 13:5,6; The thorny soil, Matthew 13:7; The good soil, Matthew 13:8.

Explain: **During this series we're going to be studying some of the stories Jesus told in the book of Matthew to teach us how to live as His followers. When Jesus talked to people about things that were hard to understand, He often used stories called parables. That way, even though the things He was saying were hard to understand, the people hearing what He had to say would be able to grasp at least part of what He was saying. In today's story Jesus used an interesting parable to communicate a powerful truth.** Ask for 10 volunteers to help act out the parable in Matthew 13:1-9. Assign students the following roles: "Farmer"; "Seeds"; four "Soils" (one volunteer for each of the four soil signs you prepared); "Bird"; "Sun" and "Thorns" (you'll need two volunteers to be thorns). **Note:** It's OK if some students play more than one role.

Ask the actors to act out their roles with as much dramatic feeling as possible as you slowly read Matthew 13:1-9; then discuss the following:

Who does the farmer represent? God.

What do the seeds represent? God's Word, the truths that He's trying to show us.

What are the differences between the four types of soil? They were different in their willingness to receive or hear the truth that God was trying to give them.

Read Jesus' explanation of this parable from Matthew 13:18-23 and ask:

What do you think Jesus wanted His listeners to learn from this parable? It's important to listen to God and allow Him to change our hearts to become more like His. We need to prepare the "soil" of our hearts to receive His Word and allow it to grow.

What things might be considered rocks or thorns in our lives? Sin, distractions or being too busy to spend time with God.

As you close this option, help students understand the importance of removing the things in our lives that keep us from hearing God.

Option 2  Chat Room

You'll need Several Bibles, copies of "Getting the Latest Dirt" (p. 23), pens or pencils and candy.

Explain: **Many times when Jesus wanted to get across a big idea that might have been too difficult for people to understand, He used a parable. A parable is a story that communicates a truth in a way that people can understand.** Ask for volunteers to read Matthew 13:1-23 to the group, but don't explain the parable until after the following activity:

Distribute "Getting the Latest Dirt" and pens or pencils. Explain to students that you want them to ask a different student in the room one question each from the handout. If you have a small class, make sure that adults get in on the action. Give candy to students as they finish their interview questions.

When students are done interviewing, have them gather in the center of the meeting room and sit down. Ask students to share the answers they collected on their handouts. Be sure the following questions are discussed:

What does Jesus mean when He speaks about soil? He's making an analogy. The soil is supposed to be our hearts.

What does the seed represent? God's Word, God's voice.

What is Jesus trying to communicate to His hearers? God wants us to listen to Him. God wants us to be open to what He has to say to us and obey Him.

Why should we listen to God? Because God loves us and is the source of our lives. He wants only good things for us and from us.

Explain: **God strongly desires not only to speak to us, but He also longs for us to listen to what He says. The key to communicating with God is removing the**

Option 3  Pulse Points

things in our lives that prevent us from hearing what He has to say to us.
You'll need Your Bible, a baking pan (or any container that can simulate a farmer's field), small rocks, dirt and thorns (if you can't find thorns, use candy corn as a substitute).

> **Note:** You may use the farmer's field items again in Step 4, Option 3: Spread the Fire.

Bible Bonus Note (Cont'd.)

each strip for walking. As farmers walked, this ground became packed as hard as pavement. This is the ground that Jesus calls "the wayside."
• It was common for the soil in Palestine to have a layer of stone underneath. When Jesus refers to the stony ground, He's probably referring to this type of soil over stone.

The Big Idea
God wants us to listen to Him and He has made it possible for us to listen to Him.

The Big Question
What do we have to do to listen to Him?

Begin by explaining: **Most would agree that we need to be open to listening to God. But what does it take to listen to God? Jesus used stories to make some very** confusing stuff understandable. He often told stories called "parables" to help people understand the things about God and His kingdom that would be difficult to grasp. In this parable Jesus shows us two things we need to do if we want to listen to what God has to say to us.

1. Be prepared.

Read Matthew 13:1-23. Explain: **One of the noticeable things is that only one of the soils that Jesus mentions is well-prepared soil because it's the well-prepared soil that actually yields a harvest.** Ask: **What can we do to prepare our hearts so we'll hear God?** Read the Bible, pray, sing, confess sin, etc.

Explain that you'd like to look at this the way a farmer would. Invite a student to come up and put dirt in the pan while another student adds the thorns and rocks. Ask: **If you're a farmer, would you want to plant stuff in this?** Explain that Jesus wants us to prepare to listen to him by removing rocks and thorns that hinder our spiritual lives. With each response from students of what they think these things might be, remove a thorn or rock from the "field."

2. Listen.

If you used Option 1 in Step One, remind students about the experience of trying to hear someone when the background noise is unbelievably loud. If you did not use Option 1 in Step One, explain to students how difficult it is to understand people when you can't hear them. Try this simple object lesson for getting the point across. Have everyone stand up and walk to the other side of the room, face away from you and have loud conversations with each other. Then, speaking in a quiet voice, give students simple directions to hop on one leg back to where they were standing.

Point out how many people did it because they heard you and how many did it because they saw their friends doing it. Help students understand that we've got to listen for God's voice so we can do what *He* asks, not so we can follow what our friends might hear.

This step helps students understand how they can listen to God in their daily lives.

Option 1

Chat Room

You'll need Butcher paper or newsprint, pens or pencils and masking or transparent tape.

Ahead of time, ask several people on your church staff or several close friends to respond to the statement "What does it mean to listen to God?" Then write their answers on separate large sheets of butcher paper or newsprint and tape them to the walls of the meeting room.

Explain that you want students to vote in the next few minutes. Point out the statements and ask them to move to the statement that they agree with the most. When they have all decided, have a few of them at each statement share why they've chosen that statement. Then ask students to gather at the statements that they least agree with and discuss with the whole group why they disagree.

Divide students into groups of three or four and instruct them to think of a new way they could listen to God. Explain: **We all know that we can listen to God in prayer. I'd like for you to think of *other* ways we can listen to God, like walking on the beach or sitting quietly in your room with the radio turned off. Be creative.**

Allow groups a few minutes to brainstorm, then have each group create a freeze-frame picture that shows their idea in action—without saying out loud what the picture is. For example, if students think up the idea of walking at the beach as a way to listen to God, include one person walking, another person as the sun and the third person as a wave. When a group has made their presentation, have the other groups guess what they are acting out. **Option:** If you are short on time, you could have each group share their best idea.

Option 2 — Real Life

You'll need Copies of "Learning to Listen" (p. 24) for every five students.

Introduce this section by explaining: **Listening to God is a daily thing. We're going to look at three daily occurrences in the lives of people who might be hearing God speak to them.** Have students form groups of five; then distribute "Learning to Listen." Ask each group to choose (or you assign) one of the three situations to discuss. Instruct groups to create a simple role-play that would finish these situations; then have each group act out their response.

Option 3 — Tough Questions

You'll need Your Bible and an open heart to ask yourself these questions before you ask them of students.

1. **How does God speak—in a voice that we can actually hear or in other ways?** We know from Scripture that He has spoken in an audible voice and that He still continues to, but most of the time we probably won't hear an actual voice. He also speaks to us through Scripture, a pastor's message, a friend's, parent's or teacher's advice, etc.

2. **Why do some people hear an actual voice when God speaks to them and others do not?** It's tough to know exactly why God speaks in different ways to different people. Some factors might be the person's openness to God, the urgency of the message, the certainty that God wants to communicate, and just God's own plan, which we might never be able to fully understand.

3. **If God is so powerful, why doesn't He just break in, interrupt our lives and *tell* us what He wants us to know?** Occasionally He does break into our lives and speak directly to us, as He did to Moses, Abraham and others. But mostly He "speaks" in quiet ways because He loves us and He wants us to learn to listen much like a lost child listens for a parent's voice.

4. **What is the best way to clear out all the junk in our lives so we can hear God?** The best way is to ask God to show us the things that are interfering with our ability to hear Him and then remove them! Another good idea is to read the Bible and see what it says about things that get in between us and God. Read Psalm 15:1-5 and Psalm 119:97-104 to find out more.

5. **How do we know if it's really God who is trying to get our attention?** Great question. Lots of people have gotten into trouble because they've thought it was God speaking to them, but it probably really wasn't. Three things you can do if you're not sure: Keep praying about it, talk to wise friends and adults to see what they think, and see if it matches up with what God's Word teaches us about the things He wants us to do.

STEP 4 — MOVING OUT

This step helps students commit to having their spiritual ears prepared to hear from God.

Option 1 — Light the Fire

You'll need Popsicle sticks and fine-tipped felt pens.

Hand each student a popsicle stick and a pen. Explain: **Listening to God can be so difficult, especially when there are other distractions going on in our lives. I'd like you to think about things that interfere with your ability to listen to God.**

Ask students to write one thing on their sticks that disrupts their ability to hear God. Answers may include their busy schedules, their friends or their lack of desire. Collect the sticks, and toss them all in the air, letting them fall to the floor. Ask students to grab one of the sticks that isn't theirs and read it to themselves. Explain that you want them to pair up and come up with a solution to the problem that's written on the stick.

Explain that the best way to hear God is by having a personal relationship with Him. Share how your personal relationship with Jesus has affected your life. Give students

Youth Leader Tip

Junior highers (and many adults!) are hesitant to make tough decisions in front of their friends they are more likely to take the plunge if they see others making big choices. If you have other adult leaders or volunteers, ask them to respond, too. If you are the sole adult, you should respond. Seeing adults admit to these rocks or thorns will encourage students to be more comfortable with responding.

Youth Leader Tip

It is very important to follow up with students about any results they experience as a result of their prayers. If you can't touch base with them during the week, set aside a time at the next meeting to ask if anyone has had an answer to their prayers of the week before.

the opportunity to ask Jesus to be their Savior, take over their lives and speak to them just as a best friend would.

Option 2 — Fired Up

You'll need Zipporino!

Remind students that God wants us to listen to Him. He wants our hearts to be open and ready to hear what He has to say. If possible, share a story about a time when you really needed to hear God's voice or needed to change some things in your life to help students to start thinking about the choice they're about to make.

Explain that the left side of the room is the "I need to listen" side for people who don't have many things in their lives that might distract them from hearing God—they just need to listen. The right side of the room is the "I need to clean house" side for people who have some work to do before they will be able to listen. They need to get rid of the rocks and thorns that distract them from listening to or even recognizing God's voice.

Assure students that they're *not* being graded on their spirituality or their relationship with God. Turn off (or dim) the lights. Instruct students to walk to whichever side of the room describes them best. If students aren't sure, have them stand in the center.

Explain that they've made a commitment to God, and it's up to them to keep the commitment they've made. Spend the next several minutes allowing students to pray aloud for each other in pairs where they are standing. Then close the meeting with prayer, asking God to encourage students as they strive to listen to what He wants to say to them.

Option 3 — Spread the Fire

You'll need Sunflower seeds, a baking pan or any container that can simulate a farmer's field filled with dirt (if you did Option 3 in Step 2, you're already prepared) and a live worship music team or a CD of worship music.

Explain: **Just as there are things that keep those of us who have asked Jesus to take over our lives from hearing God, there are also things in our friends' lives that keep them from hearing and following Christ. Prayer is the most important thing we can do to help our friends be open to hearing the message that Jesus is our Savior.**

Distribute one sunflower seed to each student, explaining that the seeds represent their commitment to pray that their friends who aren't Christians yet would become more open to hearing the seeds of God's Word. Place the pan with dirt in the front of the room. Ask students to identify one friend who needs the thorns or rocks removed from his or her life in order to receive God's truth. Ask students to pray silently for that friend while they are sitting; when they are done praying, have them come to the front of the room and place their seeds in the pan. Have worship music playing as students come forward.

Getting the Latest Dirt

1. Ask one person one of the following questions (your choice):

   Who do you think represents the farmer in the story?

   What do you think the seeds stand for in the story?

2. Find another person and ask him or her to answer one of these two questions:

   What do you think is the meaning of the rocky soil?

   Why does Jesus call some soil "rocky"?

3. OK, you're probably tired, but ask another person one of the following questions:

   Why does Jesus use the example of thorny ground?

   What do the thorns represent?

4. You're not done yet! Ask another person—well, you know the drill:

   What do you think the hard ground on the path represents?

   Who do you think the birds represent?

5. Finally! This is it! Ask one last person one of the following three questions:

   Jesus talks about "good soil." What do you think good spiritual soil is?

   Why is being good soil so important?

   How do you like answering a bunch of questions?

Learning to Listen

Situation One

Lately you've been feeling very out of it—especially at church. When you're there, you feel like they're talking way over your head. It doesn't seem to mean anything to you. And when you read your Bible, you feel like it's written in another language.

And yet you distinctly remember a time when you knew God very well. While you don't consider yourself a spiritual rocket scientist, you're realizing more and more that you don't even remember what God's voice sounds like. You're beyond nervous and approaching worried. Life-changing questions begin creeping up: Why do I feel so out of touch at church? Why do I feel so distant from God?

Discuss:

How should this person get back in touch with God?

How should this person begin listening to God?

Situation Two

You're approached by Jim, Steve and Mary—and they look like they want to talk. You aren't really surprised. The assault begins.

Mary starts in, "Hey, we've been missing you at church lately."

"Yeah, I know. I just feel so bad about going back."

"I wouldn't give it a second thought. I think they've forgotten about when you overflowed the toilet in the restroom. I think they knew you were just goofing off. I wouldn't worry about it."

"OK. Well, maybe."

"So, why won't you come back? You know we're having that all-nighter this weekend."

"I just don't know. It's just that ever since that whole thing, I feel like I'm not cut out for church. I think all that heaven stuff is neat, but it doesn't really have anything to do with my life."

Discuss:

Do you think this person should consider these friends as God speaking to him? Explain.

How would you advise this person about listening to God?

Situation Three

Last night you had the weirdest dream that seemed so real.

You dreamed that you were with God in a hallway and He was carrying you. As He held you, you began firing questions at Him about everything you could think of. And the cool thing was that He had the perfect answer to every question you asked. Your last memory in the dream was Him saying to you, "Stand firm, and tell people about me." Then you woke up.

Well, you did what you thought God told you to do. You told your older brother. After he finished laughing uncontrollably, he said, "You're nuts. No one can hear God no matter how hard they listen."

So the ball is in your court. How will you respond to him? Is it true that you can actually hear God? How will you explain that to him?

Discuss:

Are dreams a real way God speaks to us?

Devotions in Motion

WEEK ONE: LISTENING TO GOD: THE SOWER

DAY 1

Fast Facts

Get into 1 John 5:1-4 to see if God's commandments are heavy or light.

God Says

Every night Evan had to clean the kitchen. On Thursday Evan and his mom had a great day together—they rented a video and made sundaes for dessert. That night Evan finished cleaning the kitchen in 20 minutes. The next day Evan fought with his mom over using the phone and was so busy thinking about how unfair his mother was that it took him an hour and a half to clean the kitchen.

Lots of times it's easier to obey someone and do the right thing when you remember how much you love the person in charge.

I Do

Doing what God wants you to do is way easier to do when you're in love with him. What are two things that would be different in your week if you were in love with God?

Pray that God will help you love him more today.

Pulse

FOLD HERE ---

DAY 4

Quick Questions

See how fast you can find 1 Corinthians 11:1. Time yourself and find out whose example you should be following.

God Says

If you were lost at Disneyland and could only follow one person to an exit, who would you follow? Would it be...

☐ The girl selling churros and frozen lemonade?

☐ A four-year-old crying for his blankie?

☐ Your mom or dad?

☐ A person dressed up in a Donald Duck suit who can't see very well?

Why would you follow that person?

I Do

In this life, why is Jesus the right person to follow?

What do you think He might lead you to do today?

Quick Questions

Run—don't walk!—To 2 Timothy 1:7 and discover some of The Things God's given you.

God Says

If you were going To dissect a frog in science class, which of These Tools would your Teacher give you?

- [ ] White lab coats To keep The muck off
- [ ] A box of 50 blue ballpoint pens
- [ ] A scalpel and Tweezers
- [ ] A hairbrush

I Do

According To 2 Timothy 1:7, What Tools has God given you To help you follow Him?

I Do

What are some of The ways you can use The Tools God has given you Today?

FOLD HERE

Fast Facts

Flip To Psalm 119:66-168 To find out how much God knows about you.

God Says

Mai was supposed To be vacuuming her mother's bedroom. But she wasn't. She was poking around in her mother's makeup putting lipstick on her eyelids and mascara on her mouth. She dug in The dresser drawer and found her mother's favorite necklace. As she went To put iT on, she looked in The mirror and saw her mother standing behind her, watching her with her arms crossed.

God is a lot like The parent with eyes in The back of His head. The only difference is That God really does know all about you and He knows what's best for you.

I Do

The best way To let God Take care of you is To obey His commandments. He has given us These commandments To protect us. He knows you better than anyone—and He loves you better than anyone!

What is one of His commandments That you could obey Today That you didn't obey yesterday?

The Big Idea

A little faith goes a long way.

Session Aims

In this session you will guide students to:

- See that even little faith makes a big difference;
- Feel comforted knowing that they can accomplish great things if they have faith;
- Choose one area in their lives where they'd like to have more faith.

The Biggest Verse

"I tell you the truth, if you have faith as small as a mustard seed…. Nothing will be impossible for you." Matthew 17:20

Other Important Verses

Matthew 17:14-21; Hebrews 11:1,2; James 1:2-4

Faith: The Mustard Seed

STEP 1
MOVING IN

This step gets students thinking about some ways that faith makes a difference.

Option 1  Move It

You'll need Your Bible.

As students arrive, welcome them and divide them into groups of four, then whisper *one* of the following phrases to each group: "Someone who has to trust something that can't be seen," "Someone who is hoping for something really big," "Someone who's taking a big risk." When every group has been assigned one situation, explain: **I've just given you a situation that I'd like you to create a silent skit for. Your skits must be about someone who is dealing with whatever situation I whispered to your group. You can use whatever you'd like to get across the idea of the skit *except* your voices.** Allow groups several minutes to create their skits, then have them present their silent skits. As each group finishes, ask its members to share the situation they acted out. When all groups have finished, ask: **How do these situations describe faith? Is it easy for you to trust a power that you can't see?**

Explain that the word "faith" sounds simple, but actually it's pretty complicated. Read Hebrews 11:1 and transition to the next step: **Today we're going to discuss what faith is. Even though we can't see faith, we can sure see what it does in our lives.**

Option 2 📱 Chat Room

You'll need Several Bibles, large sheets of newsprint or poster board, masking or transparent tape and several felt-tip pens.

Ahead of time, write the following statements on the sheets of paper; then hang the papers on the wall in various locations around the room:

- All of us get faith as a gift when we give our lives to Christ.
- Jesus only intended some of us to be able to do amazing things with faith.
- Since you really can't see faith, it doesn't exist.
- Jesus was able to do miracles, but He doesn't expect that we will be able to do them.

As students arrive, welcome them, have them form groups of three and give each group a felt-tip pen. Instruct students to walk to each statement and write whether they—as a group—agree or disagree with the statement and why. When all groups have had a chance to write their responses, ask students to leave their groups and go to the statement that they feel they individually agree with the most. After students have chosen their statements, give these new groups (standing at each statement) five minutes to come up with a way to defend that statement.

When groups are finished, have them present their defenses and be sure to congratulate everyone on their hard work. Then read Hebrews 11:1 (questions are based on the *New King James Version*). Discuss: *What is faith? Read Hebrews 11:1*

What does it mean when it says that faith is "the substance of things hoped for"?

What does it mean when it says that faith is "the evidence of things not seen"?

Is it difficult for you to prove something you can't see?

What does it take to believe in something that you can't see?

Explain: **Today we'll be talking about faith—something that we can't see, but we sure can see what it does in our lives.**

then finish Hebrews 11 + read extra info in Bible

Option 3  Fun and Games

You'll need Your Bible, one or two large bedsheets, paper and pens or pencils.

Ahead of time, ask five students to volunteer for a foot-identification game. Tell them that when the game starts, you'd like them to take their shoes and socks off and roll up their pants so their clothes don't show beneath the sheet they'll be standing behind.

Greet students and instruct them to gather at one end of the meeting room. Distribute a piece of paper and a pen or pencil to each student. Ask two students or adult leaders to volunteer to hold the bedsheet approximately one foot off the ground like a curtain, then explain: **We're going to play a game, but I need your cooperation. Please close your eyes and keep them shut until I tell you to open them.** When everyone has closed their eyes, ask the barefoot volunteers to enter and stand behind the bedsheet. Before you have students open their eyes, make sure that only the volunteers' feet are visible.

Ask students to open their eyes and then explain: **I'd like you to guess whose feet you're seeing under the bedsheet. I'm going to number these sets of feet from one to five. I'd like you to guess whose feet belong to each number and write down your guess.** Number the sets of feet by pointing and assigning them a number. When everyone has guessed, have the two volunteers drop the sheet. Have students check their answers by pointing out each set and asking students to stand if they guessed correctly. When everyone has shared their guesses, ask:

How many of you were sure about your guesses?

What made you sure about your guesses?

What made this activity difficult?

What would have made it easier?

Read Hebrews 11:1. Discuss: **How does this game relate to this passage?**

Explain: **Having faith is a lot like this game. You couldn't see who was behind the sheet except for their feet. The feet were evidence of the actual person. Our faith is like that. We can't see all of God, but we can figure out how He's working. Today we're going to learn more about how to know where God is working even though we can't see Him.**

NOTES

This step helps students realize that faith, even a little faith, is important to their lives.

Option 1  Move It

You'll need Several bags of large marshmallows (20 marshmallows for every four to six students), a box or two of toothpicks (20 toothpicks for every four to six students), several Bibles, paper and pens or pencils.

Have students divide into small groups of four to six and give each group 20 marshmallows. Ask them to build the tallest tower they can, using just the marshmallows. This will be very frustrating until you hand each group 20 toothpicks; then they can really begin to build a tall tower. When they're finished, judge which tower is the tallest. Comment on the fact that although toothpicks seem to be small and unimportant, they make the marshmallow towers possible.

Next read Matthew 17:14-21 and explain: **The amazing thing that Jesus does in this passage is heal this boy. But the point of it is that Jesus wants us to understand how essential faith is in the life of the believer. I'd like you to imagine for a moment that you are present in this situation.**

Assign each small group one of the following people to represent: The boy's father; the disciples; part of the multitude; the boy. Give each group paper and pens or pencils. Have groups write a first-person story based on their assigned person's perspective as Jesus heals the boy. When everyone is finished writing, have each small group read their story to another group; then bring the students together to share with the whole group what they learned about the situation in Matthew as a result of this activity.

Discuss:

What does this passage say about faith? Even a small amount of faith can do what seems impossible to us.

How are we supposed to show faith? By putting our trust in Jesus' power to accomplish great things.

What is difficult about doing the miraculous things that Jesus says we can do? They are seemingly impossible and we know we can't do them on our own. But the Bible is full of the miraculous things God did when someone had a little faith.

What are the essential ingredients for faith? Trust. Hope.

Why does Jesus equate faith to the size of a mustard seed? He wants us to understand that we need just a little faith to do great things. A mustard seed is very small and yet it can grow into a huge bush.

Explain: **Faith is an interesting thing. We can't see it, but we can see the effects of it. It was impossible to "see" the faith that Jesus had to be able to heal the boy, but the effects of His work were obvious. Jesus told us that if we'll have faith, we can do amazing things. He promised us that nothing would be impossible for us if we have faith. So let's go deeper into this subject. I'd like us to focus on how we can have faith—even when we can't see it.**

Chat Room

You'll need Several Bibles, vegetable oil, a clear glass half full of water, one-fourth cup of salt and a small bottle of food coloring.

Ahead of time, practice this "experiment" to be able to talk about it and perform the actions at the same time.

Gather students in the center of the room and explain: **Little things can make a big difference and I've got a little experiment today to prove it.**

Show the glass of water. Pour some vegetable oil on the water and allow it to separate from the water. Next, put two drops of food coloring into the water and wait for it to drop out of the oil and into the water. Explain: **A little bit of food coloring can make a big difference in the water.** Next, sprinkle salt on the top of the oil, making sure to distribute the salt evenly over the surface of the oil. Allow time for the salt to sink the oil to the bottom, and the oil to rise to the surface again. Then ask: **How would you explain what you are seeing?** A little bit of salt or a little bit of food coloring makes a big difference.

Point out that Jesus explained that even a little bit of faith could make a big difference. Read Matthew 17:14-21. Discuss:

What would you be thinking if you were a disciple and you saw this happen?

What would you think if you were the boy?

What if you were the boy's parents?

If you were a disciple, would you want to be able to do what Jesus did?

Read Matthew 17:20, 21 again and ask:

Why does Jesus compare faith to a mustard seed? Because a mustard seed is very small, but it can grow into a huge bush. Jesus wants us to understand that all we need is a small amount of faith to do great things for God and our faith will grow.

Why do you think Jesus used the example of moving a mountain to show the power of faith? Because He wants us to know that even big things are no problem if we have faith.

Explain: **Imagine hearing Jesus' words for the first time. Wouldn't your reaction be one of wonder and amazement? Imagine hearing Him tell you that you could move mountains. Faith might be invisible, but the effects of faith in our lives are certainly clear to see. God has called us to have faith and next we're going to figure out together how to use it.**

Pulse Points

You'll need Your Bible, vegetable oil, a clear glass half-full of water, one-fourth cup of salt and food coloring.

The Big Idea
Even a little faith can move mountains.

The Big Question
Will we trust God to do big things with our little faith?

Explain to students that you want them to repeat the following sentence after you: "Even a little faith can move mountains." Have students repeat it after you several times, then explain that you're going to help them understand what this sentence means in two parts.

NOTES

1. Small Faith

Read Matthew 17:20,21 to the group. Point out: **Jesus mentions that a little faith goes a long way. Jesus wants us to understand that if we'll have faith, we can do great things. He uses the analogy of the mustard seed because He wants us to grasp the idea of a small amount of faith.**

Illustration: Pour the oil into the water and allow it to separate and rise to the top, then add a few drops of food coloring and watch as it colors the water. Explain that just a little bit of food coloring can make a big difference.

2. Moving Mountains

Ask students to think of one impossible thing that they would love to see God do. Some examples might be helping their family with money problems or healing a sick aunt. Then tell students that the impossible thing is their "mountain." Tell them that God *loves* to do the impossible in their lives, but their faith plays a part in this. Read Matthew 17:14-18 to show how Jesus highlights the role of faith.

Illustration: Remind students that even a little faith can make a difference. Then shake the salt into the glass and watch as the salt carries the oil to the bottom. When the salt dissolves, the oil is allowed to rise to the top. The salt represents the power of faith to change whatever is happening in our lives.

STEP 3 — MOVING ON

This step helps students get a grasp on how to put their faith into practice in their own lives.

Option 1 — Chat Room

You'll need Several Bibles and copies of "Faith in the Real World" (pp. 36-37).

Explain: **All this faith we've been talking about can be somewhat difficult to have. To make it easier, I'd like you to consider how you can have faith when you're in the middle of a crisis.**

Divide students into three groups and assign each group one of the situations from "Faith in the Real World." Ask the groups to read their situations and discuss how they could exercise faith in that situation. Allow enough time for each group to prepare their explanation; then have them share their situations and ideas with the whole group.

Discuss: **Does God expect that we'll always be successful in living our faith and performing miracles?** He'd like us to be full of faith, but He knows that we all fail at times. (**Suggestion:** Give a personal example of how your own faith has faltered.) Whenever we lack faith, we can ask Him to give us faith. **What should we do when we feel like we have faith but nothing happens?** Keep praying and trusting God to

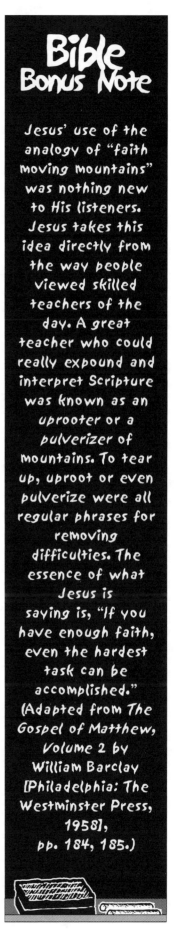

Bible Bonus Note

Jesus' use of the analogy of "faith moving mountains" was nothing new to His listeners. Jesus takes this idea directly from the way people viewed skilled teachers of the day. A great teacher who could really expound and interpret Scripture was known as an uprooter or a pulverizer of mountains. To tear up, uproot or even pulverize were all regular phrases for removing difficulties. The essence of what Jesus is saying is, "If you have enough faith, even the hardest task can be accomplished." (Adapted from *The Gospel of Matthew, Volume 2* by William Barclay [Philadelphia: The Westminster Press, 1958], pp. 184, 185.)

Reaching beyond this study and into students' lives can be a daunting task. After all, they live very real, very busy lives. And sometimes either they, or their parents, may not be pleased at seeing you on their doorstep (especially at dinnertime!). So how do you get involved in their lives outside of regular meetings or events?

Hang out. Whether it's a sports field or a pizza place, go where you know they hang out. Seeing you and maybe even talking with you might just be what they need.

Creatively contact. Do you have E-mail? Do they? Use it. Or get another student you know well to leave a note in their locker from you.

Get involved. Junior high and middle schools are always looking for chaperones, coaches, tutors, hall or lunchroom supervisors and teachers' aides. Get involved in a project that you know students are involved in.

do what is best. If we have faith that God will do something, such as giving us the latest, greatest bike, when that's not His will, then He won't do it. But He will do and give what is best for us.

Option 2 — Real Life

You'll need Several Bibles.

Introduce this step by asking students to listen to a story that shows us how to have faith.

Many years ago, a weary traveler hiked for miles across the desert with the hot sun beating down on him. His water supply was gone and he knew that if he didn't find water soon to quench his thirst, he would surely die.

In the distance, he spotted a deserted cabin which gave him hope that maybe water was to be found there. He made his way to the cabin and discovered an old well. He frantically pumped the handle of the well to draw water, but all that came from the pump was dust.

Then he noticed a tin can tied to the pump, with a note inside. The note said: "Dear stranger: This pump is all right as of June 1932. I put a new sucker washer in it, and it should last for quite a few years. But the washer dries out and the pump needs to be primed. Under the white rock, I buried a jar of water, out of the sun and corked up. There's enough water in it to prime the pump, but not if you drink some first. Pour about one-fourth of the water into the pump and let her soak for a minute to wet the leather washer. Then pour the rest quickly and pump hard. You'll get water. Have faith. This well has never run dry. When you get watered up, fill the bottle and put it back as you found it for the next stranger who comes this way. Pete"[1]

Discuss:
Would you have poured the water into the pump or drunk the water? Why?
Why is it difficult to have faith in something that we can't see?

What does this story tell you about faith? Sometimes you might have to do something or trust something that seems unrealistic or just plain dumb before you get results.

Explain: **Having faith means that we trust God no matter what. Sometimes believing that God wants to use us to do miraculous things is like pouring out water without knowing if our experiment will work.** Help students get a broader view of what the Bible says about faith by having them read Hebrews 11:1 and James 1:5-8.

Option 3 — Tough Questions

You'll need Your Bible and these questions.

Ahead of time, prepare for this step by studying Hebrews 11:1,2 and James 1:2-4.

1. **Imagine that a friend from church comes to you and is really confused because she had faith that her cousin would not have cancer; then it turned out that he did. What would you say to her?** God's timing is

usually different from ours, so we should continue to pray. Our faith will never override His will, so there are some things that even great faith cannot accomplish outside of God's will for us.

2. **If Jesus promises these types of results from having faith, why aren't more spiritual mountains being moved?** It's difficult to have this level of trust in God. Also, God may have a plan with a certain time schedule that might mean it will take a little longer for those spiritual mountains to be moved.

3. **If we have faith that God will give us a new computer, would God give it to us? Why or why not?** Not necessarily, He will only give us what is best for us. There are times we want things that are not the best for us or that we don't need and God knows that, so He doesn't allow us to have everything we want. But He does bless us with everything we need plus many extra blessings besides.

4. **What are some things that we can do to build our faith?** We can study our Bibles and see how God has acted in the past. And we can talk to each other or family members to see how God continues to act today.

STEP 4
MOVING OUT

This step helps students choose one area in their lives where they want to have more faith.

Option 1 — Light the Fire

You'll need A VCR, a TV and the video *Flubber,* with Robin Williams.

Ahead of time, cue the video approximately 30 minutes from the beginning to the scene in which Williams puts the Flubber in his back pocket and falls out the window. You'll use this clip to help students understand what it means to have faith.

Explain: **Having the type of faith that Jesus talks about requires trust in God. If we can trust that God really means what He says, then having this type of faith will become more of a reality for us.**

Show the clip from *Flubber,* then explain that Robin Williams's character knew he could count on the Flubber to save him. Continue: **We can count on God. The beginning of a faith-filled life is to accept the gift of salvation God gives to us through Jesus. If we can trust Him to forgive our sins and make us His own children, then we can trust Him to watch over our whole lives as well. Some of us need to take this**

first step of faith today and ask Him to be our Savior. That means we recognize that we can't trust in ourselves and need to trust in Him to take over our lives. As you bow your heads, I want to lead you through this prayer and if you want to ask Jesus to come into your life for the first time, you can repeat this prayer after me:

> Dear Jesus, I have faith that You are the only true Savior, and I give You my life today. I believe You lived a perfect life, died to bear the punishment for my sins and that God has raised You from the dead. Help me to trust You from this moment forward as my Lord and King. Amen.

Note: For further student information regarding salvation and making a commitment to Jesus, see the "It's Your Move" student article on pages 95-96 in *Christianity: The Basics* by Kara Eckmann Powell (Gospel Light, 1999).

Transition to a second time of prayer by stating: **Some of you have already made that decision and today you need to take a different step of faith.** Have all students bow their heads. Ask students to think about their level of trust in God and explain that you want to give them a chance to commit to really trusting God for one specific area in their lives that is right now causing them a lot of worry and stress. If students are interested in doing this, ask them to look at you. When you've allowed time for students to respond, close the meeting with a brief prayer asking God to help students have faith.

As you conclude, ask students who responded to either prayer to stay after to talk with you. At that time ask these students to share what is happening in their lives and what type of commitments they want to make. Be sure you spend extra time with those who asked Jesus to be their Savior, explaining what it means to turn from our sin and trust in God instead of ourselves.

Option 2 Fired Up

You'll need Clay or play dough, a live worship music team or worship CD and player, trash can and a large plastic trash bag.

Explain: **We've learned today that having faith is essential. I'd like you to take a moment to think of what stops you from having the type of faith that Jesus talks about.**

Distribute clay or play dough and give students time to make their clay into something that represents what they feel is a barrier that prevents them from having mountain-moving faith. When students are done, explain: **Instead of presenting your "sculptures" to the entire class, I'd like you to choose a partner and share with your partner.** Allow students a few minutes to share what their sculptures represent.

Once students have shared their sculptures, continue: **Next, I'd like you to commit this barrier to God. Tell Him that you want help removing that barrier. I'm going to give you some time to do that. If you get finished before the music stops, just sit quietly and think about what we've talked about today.** Play quiet worship music and have them pray silently.

When the music is over, have students demonstrate their commitments by coming forward, smashing their sculptures and dropping them on the floor. (**Note:** Keep peace with the custodian and place the plastic trash bag on the floor where students will be dropping the clay.) As students drop their clay, begin to form it into one huge ball. When all the clay has been dropped, throw it in the trash can as a symbol of faith that God will remove those obstacles. Close the meeting with prayer asking God to remove their obstacles.

Option 3 — Spread the Fire

You'll need A clear two-liter bottle of soda, seven clear plastic cups, a funnel and a table.

Ahead of time, set up the table and place the bottle and plastic cups on the table. Pour the contents of the soda bottle into the seven plastic cups.

Explain: **Having faith in God means we have faith that He can use us to share His good news with our friends. Sometimes we feel bad when we share with our friends and nothing happens, but the reality is that something is probably happening, even if we can't see it. Studies show that the average junior higher receives Christ after he or she has heard about Him seven times.** At this point, point to your clear bottle and explain: **The bottle represents a junior higher named Doug. First, you invite Doug to church.** Pour one glass of soda into the bottle representing Doug. **Next, Doug's aunt sends him a Christmas card that explains the gospel message.** Pour another glass of soda into Doug. Continue to pour the remaining five glasses of sodas as you add additional scenarios of how Doug might hear about Jesus, such as Doug goes to church with a new friend; Doug watches a Christian television show; one of Doug's teachers tells him that he's praying for him; Doug asks you to explain about a sticker for a Christian band that you have on your notebook; and Doug hears Christian music on your stereo and says he can't figure out what the words mean.

Now the bottle representing Doug should be full. Explain that at this point, Doug is probably ready to receive Christ as Savior. Continue: **You never know what role you're playing in Doug's process of coming to know Jesus. You may be the first or you may be the third. The important thing is to continue to have faith that God will use you.**

Close in prayer, asking students to pray in pairs for two other friends or relatives they know who don't know Christ yet. Ask them to ask God to give them faith and courage to share with these two friends.

Note
1. Wayne Rice, "The Desert Traveler" *More Hot Illustrations for Youth Talks* (Grand Rapids, MI: Zondervan Publishing House, 1995), p. 55.

NOTES

Faith in the Real World

Situation One

You've been your grandma's favorite since you were born. When you were a small child, the two of you would spend countless hours watching television game shows together competing for who could get the right answers. As you got older, your grandma was always a source of encouragement and wisdom.

Last night someone from the hospital called. It seems that as your grandma was sitting down for dinner, she began to complain of a headache and fell unconscious. Paramedics were called and they rushed her to the hospital, where it was determined that she had experienced a severe stroke. Her mental faculties are all but gone and the doctors say she only has a few days to live.

You're standing over her as she lies helpless in her hospital bed. You feel led to pray for a complete healing.

- How does Matthew 17:20,21 help you understand your role in your grandmother's healing?
- How can you have faith in the middle of this situation?
- Is it right for you to expect that she will be healed? Explain.
- If she isn't healed, what is the best attitude to have toward God?

Situation Two

Since you were five years old, your father has been an independent businessman. When he began his business, it took off immediately. The boom in his business meant that your family was able to have the best of everything. There were frequent trips to Hawaii, new cars, the latest clothes and scores of other benefits.

Well, recently his business hasn't been going so well. In fact, it's been very slow. This year your family isn't going anywhere for vacation. It looks like if things don't change, your dad will have to take on a second job at a local grocery store to make ends meet.

Tonight your dad broke all of this news at the dinner table. He says that the family needs to have faith that God will meet the needs you have.

- How might Matthew 17:20,21 help you live through this difficult time in your family?
- How can you have faith in the middle of this situation?
- If your father's business fails even more, does that mean that you didn't have enough faith? Explain.
- Read James 1:2-4. What should you completely trust God for?

36

Situation Three

Your older sister has always been the popular one in the family. She's been on the cheerleading squad since she began high school as well as the drama team at your church. She always seems to have a boyfriend. You love your sister, but you're also jealous of her popularity and abilities. You wish you could be just like her.

But you feel like the family ugly duckling. Even though you're just three years younger, you don't have the friends that she has. You aren't as smart as she is. You can't sing, dance or act like she does. Last night you sat on your bed and just cried. You want so much to be like her, but you feel so awkward and you're convinced that you'll be just a "plain old ordinary nothing" forever.

Your mom heard you crying and came in to check on you. After spilling your guts, your mom told you that you needed to trust God for what He's creating you to be. God is creating you to be something incredible (so your mom says) but that takes time.

Your mom's words are comforting, but they don't help you as much as you need them to.

- How does Matthew 17:20,21 help you wait on God?
- How can you have faith in the middle of this situation?
- If you don't turn out like your sister, is it because you didn't have enough faith?
- Read James 1:2-4. What should you completely trust God for?

Devotions in Motion

WEEK TWO: FAITH: THE MUSTARD SEED

DAY 1

Quick Questions

Read Mark 9:14-29 and find out what's possible!

God Says

Your grandma has had cancer for as long as you can remember. Every night at dinner your mom prays that God will heal her. After all these years, you're getting tired of hearing that prayer. If God was going to heal her, wouldn't He have done it already?

One night as you're staring at some tuna casserole and hearing your mom pray the same prayer for Grandma, you realize how wrong you have been. If you decided that you wanted to pray with the same kind of faith that your mom does, should you...

- ☐ Sleep with your Bible under your pillow so that faith can drift into your mind?

- ☐ Make up a song about faith that you sing under your breath as much as possible?

- ☐ Decide to change your name to faith as a constant reminder of your need for faith (this would be especially powerful if you are a guy)?

- ☐ Ask God for it?

I Do

The example of the father who confessed to Jesus, "I believe! Help my lack of faith!" pretty much answers the question. If you don't feel like you have faith when you pray, whether it be for your sick grandma or your neighbor who doesn't know Jesus yet, you can ask God for it. In His timing, He'll give it to you. Then you'll see some out-of-this-world things happening around you as you pray!

FOLD HERE ----------------------------------

DAY 4

FAST FACTS

See how long it takes you to find 1 Corinthians 16:13. Try to beat your old record! It's so nice, read it twice!

God Says

When Mark started mowing Mrs. Barnfather's lawn he wanted to know exactly how she wanted it done. Did she want the edges trimmed and the flower beds weeded? Did she want him to come every week or every other week? Did she want him to pull the dandelions out or did she want him to spray EZ-Weed-B-Gone on them? He asked her a billion questions and wrote down her answers on a little piece of paper.

When Mark became a Christian, he looked at the big, thick Bible and had a billion more questions than he had ever had for Mrs. Barnfather.

I Do

Today's verse is a super-short version of how a Christian should behave. Jesus thinks our faith is one of the most important things we can help to grow. Pray that He will help you have a solid faith in Him today.

Fast Facts

Read Matthew 21:18-22 and be glad you're not a figless fig tree!

God Says

Maria prayed for weeks and weeks and weeks that her parents would get her a new telephone and her own phone line. Across town Clara wanted the same thing but prayed only that God's will be done. Two months passed and neither of them got her own telephone and phone line. That's not fair! Maria thought. Jesus made fig trees shrivel up, and He said I could have anything if I just had faith!

At the same time, Clara was just as disappointed at not getting the things she wanted, but because of her faith in God, she knew that God's will was the important thing.

I Do

It's easy to think that today's verses mean we can have anything we want just by having enough faith. But the more faith in God you gain, the more you will want to follow God's will.

Take two minutes to pray about one hard or confusing area of your life, asking that God's will be done.

Quick Questions

Race to Romans 1:1-5 to find out what comes with faith.

God Says

Imagine you're rock climbing for the first time, except T...

* You ignored the directions on your harness, so it's tied on loose and sloppy.
* You were told by the instructor to wear a helmet, but you decided it looked lame.
* You wore flip-flops instead of rock-climbing shoes.
* You skipped the beginning rock-climbing lesson, so you could sleep in.

How high do you think you would try to climb? How well do you think you would do?

I Do

How is not doing what God wants for you like being unprepared for rock climbing?

What do you need to do to be prepared to climb with God today?

FOLD HERE

The Big Idea

God has given us some amazing talents that He wants us to use to help others.

Session Aims

In this session you will guide students to:

- Recognize the importance of using their gifts;
- Feel encouraged that they have more gifts than they realize;
- Commit to using the gifts that God has given them to help others this week.

The Biggest Verse

"Well done, good and faithful servant! You have been faithful with a few things; I will put you in charge of many things. Come and share your master's happiness!" Matthew 25:21

Other Important Verses

Matthew 25:14-30; Romans 12:4-8; 1 Peter 4:10,11

Gifted by God: The Talents

STEP

MOVING IN

This step gets students thinking about all the different kinds of talents that people have.

Option 1 — Move It

You'll need Just this book.

Welcome students and explain that they're going to play "Would You Rather Be?" As you read a pair of choices, students will move to the side of the room that indicates their choice. If they'd rather be the first type of person, they should move to the left side of the room. If they'd rather be the second type of person you read about, they should move to the right side of the room.

Ask: **Would you rather be...**

A brilliant computer scientist or a fantastic fashion model?

The world's best skateboarder or the world's best snow skier?

A dancer in a football halftime show or someone who sells peanuts at halftime at the stadium?

Able to burp the alphabet or never have foot odor again?

An elementary school teacher or a writer of children's books?

The best player on your soccer team or the best student in your school?

Ask students if they can figure out what all of these have in common. The answer is that they are all talents. Explain: **A talent is a special ability and as followers of Jesus, we know that our talents are given to us by God. Today we're going to learn more about how to use our talents in the best way possible.**

Option 2 — Chat Room

You'll need A TV set, a VCR and a sports video (either a bloopers or highlights video that you can rent from your local video store).

Ahead of time, cue the video to a two- or three-minute clip that is exciting to watch.

Greet students and ask: **OK, let's say you could play any sport for the rest of your life and maybe even make some money doing it, what would you do?** Accept answers, then transition to the video by explaining that you have a video that (hopefully) shows some of those very sports.

Play the video; then discuss: **Who were the people on the video who really had talent?** These answers will probably be pretty obvious for students, including the quarterback, the pitcher, etc. Ask: **Who else was either on the video or involved with the video who had some talents?** Encourage students to keep brainstorming answers, but you may want to prompt them with some of the following: people who are supporting the athletes (the coach, the trainer, the medic, the water person) or people who make the video happen (the camera person, the person who did sound, the video editor, the producer, the graphic artist who designed the cover of the video, the person who sold or rented you the video).

Explain: **Often we focus on only certain kinds of talents, but just as we see in this video, lots of people have talents that are used to accomplish one thing. In fact, every single person has at least one talent. You may not even realize it, but you have at least one talent, and probably even more than one, that has been given to you by God to use. Today we're going to learn how to use these talents in the best way possible.**

Option 3 — Fun and Games

You'll need Paper, envelopes, pens or pencils and candy prizes for the winning team.

Ahead of time, design a team scavenger hunt related to various locations throughout the church facilities. For example, one clue could be something such as "If you've just finished playing football, you're probably going to run to this" (water fountain). Or: "If you like to read, this will be one of your favorite places" (the church library). Be sure to have 8 to 10 locations for the students to find. Put clues to each location in a separate envelope for each team. There should be enough envelopes for the number of groups of eight that you think you will have. Label each of the envelopes by team number and rearrange the order of the clues for each team so that the teams don't keep bumping into each other (or, dare we say, cheat by following each other). Distribute the clues in labeled envelopes around the church facility so that as a team reaches the correct destination, it finds another clue.

Greet students and explain that today you're going to start off with a churchwide scavenger hunt in the church. Divide students into teams of no more than eight. (**Note:** If you have a youth group of fewer than 16, just divide them in half.) Give each team a pen or pencil, a piece of paper and their first envelope. Instruct them to use the clue in the envelope to arrive at a location somewhere in the church facility. Tell them that when they reach the correct location, they'll find the clue to the next place in an envelope marked with their team number. As they arrive at each place, have students write down three ways someone could use their gifts and talents to serve God and others who come to that location. For example, if the clue leads them to the church nursery they could write down "The nursery: *caring* for babies, *teaching* them about God's love, *serving* parents by caring for their children."

Once the groups return, congratulate the winning team and discuss: **What did all of these places have in common?** They were all places where we use the special talents or abilities that God has given us. **Today we're going to learn how to use our talents, whatever they may be, in the best ways possible.**

This step teaches students that when God gives them a talent, He expects them to use it.

You'll need Several Bibles and copies of "Cool Questions" (p. 50).

Ahead of time, cut the "Cool Questions" handout into eight separate questions and tape each question to the bottom of different chairs in the room.

> **Answers to "Cool Questions":**
> 1. **God**
> 2. **Us**
> 3. **An actual talent, ability or gift**
> 4. **He congratulated them for a job well done.**
> 5. **He was ticked because the servant didn't use his one talent for any good.**
> 6. **He lost his talent.**
> 7. **Student answers will vary.**
> 8. **God wants us to use every gift He has given us, or we might lose them.**

Youth Leader Tip

How do you help junior high students feel comfortable using the gifts God has given them? Well, ever tried to rope cattle? Finding the right opportunities can be just as tough for two reasons. First, because students live in a world that tells them that they aren't old enough to be useful in God's kingdom. And second, they've believed the lie. They've grown comfortable letting others tell them that using their abilities for God's kingdom will happen *later*. Don't buy it. Help students get involved in using their abilities to glorify God now by trying the following: **Create a positive atmosphere.** Tell students you believe in them. Offer programs that get them involved in their passions. Be their advocate for using their abilities in your church and community.

Keep a file or list of things that students can do. Have a list of things that you (or others) would love to have done around the church. Keep the phone numbers of soul kitchens handy. Look for things to include in the file or list so that if a student ever asks you if there's something he or she can do to help, you're not left stammering and stuttering.

Get parents involved.

There's one group of people who believe in students more than you do their parents. Have parents tell ways you can help mobilize their kids. (They may be waiting for a chance to tell you how you should be doing your job anyway.) Hold seminars for parents that will encourage and equip them to join with you in encouraging their kids.

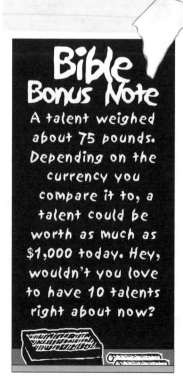

Bible Bonus Note

A talent weighed about 75 pounds. Depending on the currency you compare it to, a talent could be worth as much as $1,000 today. Hey, wouldn't you love to have 10 talents right about now?

Read Matthew 25:14-30 aloud; then explain that although a talent was a type of money in Jesus' day, today we can interpret it as a special ability or gift. Explain that you're going to play a game to help them look closer at the passage. Ask students to put their chairs in a circle, facing inward. Divide students into four different groups, labeling each group a different animal name, such as "Armadillo," "Squid," "Platypus" and "Sloth." Then have students move and find new seats, making sure that they are not sitting next to anyone else from their same animal group. Ask one student to stand in the middle of the circle and remove her chair.

Explain that the person in the middle of the circle is going to yell two or more different types of animals and the students who are in those animal groups must stand up and run to find new chairs. The person in the middle of the circle will also need to find an empty chair. The person left without a chair then stands in the middle of the circle and the process is repeated.

After a few people have been in the middle of the circle, ask students to look under their chairs for question 1. Tell students to leave all the other questions taped to the bottom of the chairs. Whoever finds question 1 must take it off the chair, stand up, read the question aloud and try to answer it. Other members of that person's same animal group may also help. Once they have answered correctly, play a few more rounds of the game, then ask students to look under their chairs for Question 2. Repeat this process until all eight questions have been answered. Conclude with the following discussion: **What does God expect us to do with talents that He gives us? What happens if we don't?**

Option 2
Chat Room

You'll need Several Bibles and a copy of "Cool Questions" (p. 50).

Ahead of time, cut the "Cool Questions" sheet into eight separate questions.

Assign five volunteers the following parts from Matthew 25:14-30: Jesus (the narrator); the master; the man with five talents; the man with two talents; and the man with one talent. Have the volunteers read Matthew 25:14-30 aloud, each playing his or her own part. When they have finished reading the passage, explain that although "talent" meant a type of money in Jesus' day, today we can interpret it as a type of skill or ability. Next, hold up the questions so that the writing is facing you and have a student choose one question. That person gets to choose another student who chooses another question, who then chooses a third student, and so on until all eight questions have been chosen.

Ask the person who has question 1 to read it, and then choose another student to answer. That student can get help from others sitting next to him.

Help students understand the answers to the questions and give them a picture of a Master who isn't out to "get" servants who aren't doing what He asks, but a Master who wants the best for us. Explain to students that this parable teaches that when God gives us talents, He has a plan for them and He expects us to use them.

Option 3  Pulse Points

You'll need Your Bible, a book or box of matches, a metal pan, a table or other surface to set the pan on and a sheet of paper.

Ahead of time, set up the table at the front of the room and place the metal pan on it.

Campfire Option: Prepare wood for a campfire or in a fireplace; then during the third point of the talk, light the fire—further illustrating the point of using your gifts to serve others.

The Big Idea

God has given us gifts and He wants us to use them to help others.

The Big Question

What do we do with the gifts that He has given us?

1. Receive the gift.

Hold up a match. Explain: **Do you think it would be okay if I started a fire in here? I think it might be kinda fun. In a few minutes we'll see how this match relates to the parable for today.**

Read Matthew 25:14-30 to the group. Ask: **Do you think this is a story about an angry master who just wants to stick it to his servants?** Explain that this master wants the best for his servants. He's not trying to catch them doing something wrong—he just wants to challenge them to use what they have been given in a responsible way. Explain that the master represents God, and the story explains what God expects us to do with the gifts He has given us.

2. Recognize the gift.

Explain: **The wicked, lazy servant didn't recognize the talent as an incredible gift that the owner had given him, so he hid his talent. The bottom line is that we need to recognize what God has given us.**

Hold up the match. Ask: **What do I have in my hand?** Students will (hopefully!) say "A match." Explain: **Well, I have an entirely different theory. I think this is just a stick with a dirty tip. I have the potential for fire in my hand, but because I don't quite understand what I have and refuse to discover what it is, I will miss out on something important. If we were cold and needed to start a fire to warm up, I have the potential to do that right here in my hand. But if I don't know what I've got, it does us no good.**

How is this match like a gift or special ability? If you don't use it, it is worthless.

3. Use the gift.

Explain: **Knowing what we've been given by God can be a huge step. But if we stop there, we run the risk of being poor stewards, or caretakers, of what we have.**

Illustration: Light the match and place it in the metal pan. As it burns, tell students all of the things that you might do with this fire. While the match slowly burns out, lead them to understand that simply lighting the match isn't enough; we have to actually use it to set something on fire before it can be useful to us.

4. Serve with the gift.

Explain: **The chief goal of the gifts that God has given us is to serve others and help them know Him. God has given us incredible gifts. These gifts have the potential to do marvelous things for God's kingdom—*if* we'll learn what gifts we have, and then use them to help others.**

Illustration: Hold up the match and the piece of paper. Light the match, then use it to light the paper. Tell students that this is exactly what we need to do with the gifts that God gives us—use them!

Note: If you are doing the **Campfire Option,** use the paper to light the wood in the campfire or fireplace. Point out how lighting the match has made it possible to start the fire that warms everyone around it.

STEP 3 — MOVING ON

This step helps students figure out how they might use their talents to serve others, especially in your youth ministry.

Option 1 — Chat Room

You'll need A life-sized replica of the Statue of Liberty—just kidding! You *will* need a comb, a shoe, an eraser and masking tape.

Greet students and ask for four volunteers. One at a time, give each of the volunteers one of the four items listed above. Explain that they are to use the given object to act out whatever you whisper in their ear while the rest of the group tries to guess what they are doing. Here are the actions you will be telling the volunteers:

- A comb being used to sweep the floor.
- A shoe being used to spread and then toss pizza dough.

- An eraser being used to clean hands.
- A piece of tape being used to handcuff a prisoner.

After volunteers have acted out all four scenarios and the rest of the students have guessed the actions, ask: **What was wrong with using these objects this way?** Explain: **We've got to figure out how to use every talent God gives us in the right way or we're going to be ineffective. Jesus' parable doesn't give a lot of specific ideas on how we're supposed to use our talents, but Paul does.** Read Romans 12:4-8 to show some of the ways we can use our talents. Discuss:

What does it mean that we "belong" to each other? It means that we are all part of the Body of Christ. **How does each ability contribute to the Body?** By serving others and helping them know more about Jesus.

Read 1 Peter 4:10,11. Ask: **How does it feel to know that you can use your gift to administer God's grace to others? What does it mean to use your gift faithfully?** It means that we must use it whenever we see a need or feel "called" to use it.

What are some gifts that can be used in our youth ministry right here and now?

Explain to students that it's essential that they discover the talents God has given them. If they are unsure about what it is, you might want to use a spiritual gifts test or some further teaching on this subject in the future. Help students understand that everything that God gives us can be used to serve others.

Option 2 — Real Life

You'll need Five copies of "The Right Equipment" (pp. 51-52) and the props listed on the script. If you are doing the variation mentioned below, you'll need 3x5-inch index cards and pens or pencils.

Ahead of time, ask four students to act out "The Right Equipment" and give them copies of the skit so they can practice their parts.

Introduce this step by explaining that the drama students are about to see represents many people's view about using the talents that God has given them.

After the drama is acted out, ask: **Which of these people did you relate to the most? When have you refused to use one of God's gifts?**

Explain that Jesus' parable doesn't give a lot of specific ideas on how we're supposed to use our talents, but Paul does. Read Romans 12:4-8. (**Note:** Make sure students understand that this is not an exhaustive list and that they might have gifts that aren't listed.) Ask:

Where does God want us to use our talents? In serving others and helping people know Jesus.

What talents has God given you?

How do you think He wants you to use them?

According to today's story, what happens if we choose not to use our talents?

Read aloud 1 Peter 4:10 and challenge: **How can you use at least one of your talents to faithfully administer God's grace to others—meaning that what you do with your gift and the way you do it shows something about who God is and how much He cares about others? How can we use our gifts to serve in our youth group?**

Variation: Hand out pens or pencils and index cards to students and ask them to write down one special talent or ability; then prayerfully consider how they could use it to serve others in the youth group.

Option 3 — Tough Questions

You'll need Your Bible and time before the study to ponder these questions.

1. **In the parable that we've studied here, we quickly see the visible results of using our talents. Do you think this is always true? Why?** Actually, no, it's not. We don't always see overnight results of using our talents. Sometimes it takes weeks, months (or even years) for us to see what God is doing as a result of our work. Our job is to be faithful and leave the results up to Him.

2. Read Romans 12:4-8, then ask, **If God loves us equally, why wouldn't He give us all the same gifts?** If we were all the same, the body would be lopsided and have way too many hands or feet. He needs a variety of people to serve in many different ways and in all kinds of places.

3. **What will happen to people who choose not to use the talents that God gives?** They'll never fully be able to do what God asks. They will not grow spiritually. They will miss out on the special blessings that come from serving God.

4. **Why doesn't God give us the gift that we want, rather than giving us something we might not want to use?** God knows us intimately. He knows what He wants us to do with our lives. Therefore, the gifts that He gives us are ultimately the best, even if we don't realize it at first. To help clarify any confusion, read 1 Peter 4:10 aloud.

Youth Leader Tip

If you don't have the time to give kids this skit in advance, try these ideas:

Make up cue cards. Assign students their parts, then ask them to read their parts off the cards. This works best if you have them read through their parts briefly before they act.

Make up "gist" cards. These are like cue cards, but are more general. You can use these along with cue cards. Make up just a few cue cards that will direct the story of the skit; then hold up the gist cards to cue actors on their emotions, movement, etc.

5. How could you use a gift God has given you to serve others, especially in our youth group?

STEP 4 — MOVING OUT

This step asks students to commit to using their talents to serve others this week.

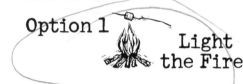

Option 1 — Light the Fire

You'll need Paper and pens or pencils.

Explain: **Since gifts that God gives us are meant, among other things, to serve others, I'd like you to think of typical situations in your everyday life where you might use a special ability that God has given you to serve others.** Divide students into groups of four. Give each group a sheet of paper and a pen or pencil and continue: **Think of typical situations that you experience every day. For example, you might list school, music practice, Bible study, eating with the family, etc. Once you've thought of a bunch of them, pick one favorite and write it on the sheet of paper.**

> **Note:** You may have to give simple airplane-folding instructions. Some may be paper-airplane-folding impaired. If you are the impaired one, ask a "talented" student to teach you and the group the art of folding one!

After they've done that, have each group fold its paper into a paper airplane. Then have groups divide into two pairs and separate to opposite sides of the room. One pair from each group of four will take the paper airplane with them. Have the pairs who have the airplanes stand on one side of the room and the pairs without airplanes stand on the other. Explain that they are going to fly their airplanes to the pairs across the room, but the pairs catching must catch a different team's airplane. If the airplane doesn't make it all the way to the other side, the throwing pair must pick it up, return to their side and throw it again. Once this is done, have groups of four return and sit together. Each group should now have another team's airplane.

Explain that finding a way to use the gifts that God has given them can feel confusing and be difficult—just like trying to catch a paper airplane. But they must keep searching for the talents that God has given them and a way to use them. Discuss the struggle to put God's gifts into practice. Explain: **Now that you have someone else's situation, think about the ways that you could put one of God's gifts into practice in that situation.** Have groups write their ideas on the paper airplanes; then invite students to share the ideas with the whole group.

Close the meeting by having students pray silently for God's help to use the talents that He has given them.

Option 2 — Fired Up

You'll need Sheets of paper, pens or pencils and meditative music (either from a CD or tape or from a live worship team).

Explain: **Just because God has given us an incredible gift doesn't mean that we have an immediate knowledge of how to use that gift or even a desire to use it. I'd like you to commit today to identifying the gifts God has given you and choosing one way you can use those gifts to serve others.**

Have students find a place alone. Play some quiet meditative music and have them contemplate the things that they've heard in today's lesson. Then distribute papers and pencils. Have students write "I think my talent is..." and "I plan on using it by..." on their papers. Then ask them to complete these statements to the best of their ability.

When they've completed their statements, have each one find a partner and share their completions with him or her. Instruct the partners to make a verbal commitment to get in touch this week to ask if they've been able to actually put their talent into practice.

When everyone has had the chance to share, have students sit in a semicircle and place their papers in front of them face down on the floor. Then ask your adult leadership team to walk around the room, praying for each student individually. When all of the students in the group have received individual prayer, close with a prayer for the whole group.

Option 3  Spread the Fire

You'll need Blank paper and felt-tip pens.

Divide students into groups of three or four. Explain: **The gifts that God gives us are meant to be used. And when they're used, they can affect people who don't know Jesus by showing them more of who Jesus is and the difference He can make in a life.** Read the following story to help them understand this point.

> I never thought that I could matter to anyone. I usually feel pretty miserable. I'm failing math and probably getting a D in science. But that's not why I feel horrible. I feel horrible because I don't have any friends. I feel rotten because no one seems to notice me. I'm tired of being a nobody.
>
> There is one person who seems to notice me. Her name is Juanita, and she's pretty nice. She keeps inviting me to go to church, but I'm not sure if I'd know anyone else there so I'd probably feel pretty stupid.
>
> But today Juanita complimented me on my new sweater (which no one else had noticed) and invited me over to play computer games at her aunt's house. I could probably do that.

Ask: **What kind of talent did Juanita have that affected this girl? What difference did it make in this girl's life? Find someone in this room that you know would make a good prayer partner with you and schedule a time this week when the two of you might call and pray about the opportunity to use your gifts in someone's life.**

When they've found partners, invite the pairs to pray together right now. Then suggest they schedule a time when they can pray together on the phone.

Youth Leader Tip

This might be an opportunity to teach students to pray for one another by having the pairs pray together. You could guide the prayer by having them repeat a prayer after you phrase by phrase, leaving space for individual names.

Youth Leader Tip

Be sensitive to students who may not know anyone in the group yet or if there's an odd number of students in the group. You could pair up students who don't know how to connect or have an adult be a prayer partner.

Cool Questions

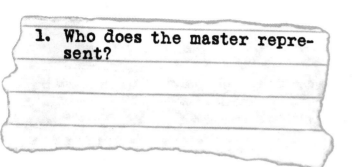

1. Who does the master represent?

2. Who do the servants represent?

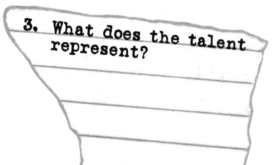

3. What does the talent represent?

4. What did the master think of the guy with five talents and the guy with two talents?

5. Why did the master get angry with the last servant?

6. What happened to the servant who didn't do anything with his talent?

7. Which servant do you relate to the most?

8. How would you summarize the meaning of this parable in one sentence?

The Right Equipment

Cast

Josh (a teenager)

Skateboarder

High School Guy (with a pair of keys)

Girl with Bike (junior high age)

Props

A toolbox, a skateboard, some coins, a set of car keys, a bike and a trash can.

Josh runs on stage carrying a large, shiny toolbox.

Josh: *(Calling backstage.)* Dad! Wait--Dad! Hold up, will ya? You spaced your tool...I said you forgot your toolbox! *(Trying to catch his breath.)* No, you forgot it. *(Stops.)* What do you mean? Wait. Time out. What do I want with this thing? No, no, Dad, it's *your* toolbox. Awww, is this one of those "You're a man now, you need your own toolbox" routines? Okay, so it's mine now. Fine. So how long you gonna be gone? Dad? Dad! *(No reply. He looks at the tool box.)* Man, this is great. He couldn't pull the old "You're a man now, you need your own 4X4" routine. *(He unlatches the toolbox.)* What am I doing? No way. I touch it and something's gonna break. Guaranteed. *(Locks it down.)* Yeah, if something happens to anything before he gets back, I'll just tell him I didn't touch a pickin' thing. That's my story.

Skateboarder enters from the opposite side of the stage carrying his skateboard. Josh picks up the toolbox and walks past the Skateboarder and tries to ignore him.

Skateboarder: Hey. Hey, dude.

Josh: What do you want? *(Keeps walking.)*

Skateboarder: Wait, wait. My wheels are starting to fall off my board. Got anything that might help?

Josh: *(Rolls his eyes, says sarcastically)* Sure. In my back pocket.

Skateboarder: *(Looking at the toolbox.)* What about the toolbox?

Josh: *(Trying to hide the toolbox behind him.)* What about it?

Skateboarder: Where did you get it?

Josh: My father. What do you care?

Skateboarder: What do you have in it?

Josh: I don't know.

Skateboarder: Ain't ya looked in it even? There might be something in there to help my wheels. Why don't you open it up?

Josh: Trust me. There's nothing that can help you in here!

Skateboarder: Maybe I could use a screwdriver or a hammer or somethin', huh?

Josh: (Shoving a coin at him.) Here's some money. Go make a phone call. I'm not opening the toolbox, okay?!

Skateboarder: (Walks away mumbling.) Why do ya carry the thing around if ya ain't gonna use it? Sheesh!

High School Guy: (Calling from offstage.) Hey, pal! Hey, buddy!

Josh turns around. He sees High School Guy with keys in his hands.

High School Guy: Hey, do you think you've got a trimensional dual-sided spanner in that box there?

Josh: Say what?

High School Guy: Hey, no, really, do you mind if I take a look? It'd really help me out. My catalytic converter is busted. (He goes to Josh, who backs away, hugging the toolbox.)

Josh: Get out. You're not looking in my toolbox.

High School Guy: Come on. That's a spiffy box there. I'm broke down, huh? One look. Okay?

Josh: Look! I'm not opening the toolbox! My dad gave it to me. It's his, got it? I'm not gonna use nothin'.

High School Guy: If your dad gave it to ya, then I'm sure he wouldn't mind.

Josh: He minds!

High School Guy: (Throws his hands up in surrender.) Okay, okay. Don't get all crazy.

High School Guy goes out. Girl with Bike comes in behind Josh. Josh sighs and turns around.

Girl with Bike: Nice toolbox. You think you got a--

Josh: No!

Girl with Bike: Maybe a wrench or some--

Josh: Nothing!

Girl with Bike: (Gestures at the box.) What's that there, then?

Josh: (Backing away.) A mistake, that's what it is. Somebody just gave it to me. I didn't know I was going to have to do something with it.

Girl with Bike: Well, hey, can I have it then?

Josh: No! It's mine! Now start walking. (Girl with Bike doesn't move.) Unbelievable. I don't need this grief. None of it! (He looks around and sees a garbage can on the other side of the stage. He goes and stuffs the toolbox in it.) That'll work. When my dad comes back, I'll go get the stupid toolbox for him. He ought to be grateful. It'll all be in one piece when he gets it. (Pauses. Wipes his hands.) Yeah, he should be real happy I took no-o-o chances with it.

JOSH taps the garbage can twice and goes out, hands stuffed in his pockets.

BLACKOUT[1]

Note

1. Adapted from Lawrence G. and Andrea J. Enscoe, "The Right Equipment" Skit'omatic (Ventura, CA: Gospel Light, 1993), pp. 74, 75.

Devotions in Motion

WEEK THREE: GIFTED BY GOD: THE TALENTS

DAY 1

Fast Facts

Merry Christmas and Happy Birthday! Read 1 Peter 4:10,11 to find out what to do with your gifts.

God Says

Lydia had the most beautiful voice and she loved to sing in front of large groups, but she refused to sing in the church choir. "Why should I sing for them?" Lydia replied when her mother asked why she never volunteered for choir. "Someone else will do it; they don't need me."

Tim was really good at playing with little kids. Every day after school he would play with his cousins and help them do their homework. When his dad asked why he didn't volunteer to help tutor kids at his school's Study Buddy program, Tim told him, "I'm just a kid! Besides, it would be hard helping kids I don't know."

I Do

God made you with special, built-in talents. But He didn't give them to you just to amuse yourself! He wants you to use them to serve and give to others the way He gave to you.

What is one gift you can use to help a friend today?

Pulse

FOLD HERE --

DAY 4

Quick Questions

Hey! Read 1 Corinthians 12:1-6 and get clued in!

God Says

Rachel, a high school student, plays the piano every week for the children's worship service. Bradley, a retired senior citizen, waters flowers every week in the church's parking lot. The senior pastor gives the sermon every Sunday. What do all of these people have in common? The answer is pretty easy—they are all using the gifts and abilities they have to serve in the church.

I Do

Think of two of your friends and figure out what gift(s) they have.

How can you encourage them to use their gifts this week?

Quick Questions

Dive headfirst into Matthew 7:11. If you're feeling brave, do a cannonball!

God Says

If you were making brownies, would you just make up how to do it or would you ask someone for a recipe?

If you wanted to fix the brakes on your youth leader's car, would you just do it or would you ask a mechanic to show you how?

If you wanted to climb the highest mountain in town, would you just walk outside one day and do it or would you ask someone who'd done it before what to take with you and which path to take?

I Do.

Do you think God wants you to start serving Him by just doing anything you can without asking Him for help? Or does He want you to ask Him first?

Ask Him to show you how to serve Him by serving one of your family members this week.

FOLD HERE --

Fast Facts

Find 1 Corinthians 12:18-20 and see what part of the body you might be.

God Says

Daniel was bummed. His brother, Aaron, played the guitar for the high school worship band each Sunday. Aaron also helped organize a concert that raised tons of money for a family who lost their house to a fire. He even started a Christian club at his public high school and got straight As and was voted vice president of his class. Aaron's so popular that people hardly ever remember Daniel's name. If they even notice him at all. They just call him Aaron's little brother.

"It's no fair," Daniel told his pastor. "Daniel's good at so much and I'm only good at working the overhead during worship!"

I Do.

Sometimes it's easy to think that the only jobs worth doing are the ones that get lots of attention. God doesn't think that's He made everyone different with different gifts to serve in lots of different places.

Pray that you'll come to know and use the gifts God gave you.

The Big Idea

Other people need to see us live out the truth.

Session Aims

In this session you will guide students to:

- Learn what Jesus says about living out their faith in the world;
- Be motivated to live their faith in their world;
- Repent of one thing in their lives that keeps them from being Christ's salt and light.

The Biggest Verse

"You are the salt of the earth....
You are the light of the world."
Matthew 5:13,14

Other Important Verses

Ezekiel 16:4; Matthew 5:13-16; 28:16-20; John 1:4; Philippians 2:12-15; James 2:14-17

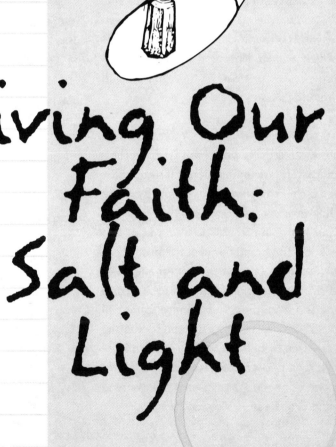

Living Our Faith: Salt and Light

STEP
MOVING IN

This step gets students thinking about how their lives can cause others to want to hear about Jesus.

Option 1 — Move It

You'll need A large paper bag, masking tape and several objects bearing a variety of commonly recognized logos, such as a hat with a Nike swoosh, a T-shirt with the CK letters for Calvin Klein, a cup with the golden arches from McDonald's, a Pepsi can with the blue and red circle, a pair of surf shorts with the Quicksilver wave, etc. You will need at least eight different items, preferably with a picture logo, not the actual company name. You may need to tape over the words on some objects. Make sure logos are ones with which your students are familiar.

Ahead of time, place the items in the paper bag to conceal them from the students.

When everyone has arrived, divide the room into two teams and explain: **Advertisers work hard to make their products immediately recognizable to the public. Sometimes they use words, sometimes simply a picture to represent their product. I want to see how well you know your logos. I'm going to pull an item out of this bag, and if you know the brand name of the product or company that the logo represents, stand up and I will call on the first person to stand. If that person is wrong then the first person from the other team to stand will get to answer.** Pull out the items one by one so that the logo can be clearly seen by both teams. Have students call out their answers. Keep track of which team correctly identifies the company or product and reward the winning team with a round of applause. Follow up by asking:

What are some other logos you can think of that weren't used in the game?

Have you ever bought a product simply because it had a certain logo? Why?

What convinced you to buy these products?

Explain: **Just as a picture can represent a product—one look and you know who made it—our lives should represent the One who made us. We are God's chil-**

dren and represent Him to the world. When people take a look at us, can they easily identify who we belong to? Today we're going to talk about being God's logo—His salt and light—in the world. Our lives should show the world that we belong to Jesus.

Option 2 — Chat Room

You'll need Just this book!

Start this chat by asking: **What is the best pizza place in town? Which athletic shoes are the coolest? What soft drink is better than any other?**

Allow students to give reasons why they feel the way they do about certain products. They should defend their answers even better than Madison Avenue because they are giving an opinion based upon their personal experience.

Ask: **What is the most convincing way to persuade someone to buy something?** Explain that the following story shows one important thing you need when you want to convince someone to buy something.

A rich Dutch merchant was seeking to buy a certain kind of diamond to add to his collection. A famous dealer in New York found such a stone and called him to come and see it.

The merchant flew immediately to New York, where the seller had assigned his best diamond expert to close the transaction. After hearing the assistant describe in perfect technical detail the diamond's worth and beauty and the clarity of its cut and color, the Dutch man decided not to buy it. Before he left, however, the owner of the store stepped forward and asked, "Do you mind if I show you that stone once more?" The customer agreed.

The store owner didn't repeat one thing that the salesman had said. Instead, he simply took the stone in his hand, stared at it and described the beauty of the stone in a way that revealed why this stone stood out from all the others he had seen in his life. The customer bought it immediately.

Tucking his new purchase into his breast pocket, the customer commented to the owner, "Sir, I wonder why you were able to sell me this stone when your salesman could not?"

The owner replied, "That salesman is the best in the business. He knows more about diamonds than anyone, including myself, and I pay him a large salary for his knowledge and expertise. But I would gladly pay him twice as much if I could put into him something I have which he lacks. You see, he knows diamonds, but I love them."[1]

Discuss:

What was the difference between the salesman and the owner of the store? One knew about diamonds, one loved diamonds.

Have you ever been around someone who was like the owner and was totally excited about what he or she had to offer?

What was that person excited about and why?

What are you or have you been so excited about that you think others would be interested in what you knew or had?

Explain: **It's easiest to tell others about something you are personally excited about. Our relationship with Jesus can't be just facts, like the salesman's in the story. We must personally experience His salvation, then we will be enthusiastic about sharing Him with others. Our own lives will make a difference in what people think of Jesus.**

Option 3  Fun and Games

You'll need A TV, a VCR and candy for prizes.

Ahead of time, record three minutes of commercials or infomercials from TV. Make up 8 to 10 trivia questions based on what happens in the video clip, such as, "What was the first person in the deodorant commercial wearing?" Be sure to write down the answers for yourself!

Greet students and divide them up into two teams (the old standby boys against girls might work here, or maybe try adult leaders against students). Ask for three volunteers from each team to be their team's representatives. Play the video clip; then ask the trivia questions. When someone knows the answer, she should raise her hand. If she answers correctly, her team gets 1,000 points. If the answer is incorrect, her team loses 1,000 points and the other team gets a chance. If the second team's volunteer doesn't know the answer, the rest of the first team gets to guess.

Once the game is over, give candy prizes to the winning team and discuss:

What are some of your favorite commercials?

What makes them your favorites?

Do you think commercials influence what you buy or maybe what your friends buy?

Explain that the most effective commercials are the ones that show how our lives will be better if we use that deodorant or this acne cream. Ask: **How are these selling points like telling people about Jesus?** The best way to tell people about Jesus is to show that our lives are different. If we are positive, loving and excited about Jesus, then maybe they'll want to try Jesus for themselves. We don't need to "sell" Jesus to others, but we do need to share Jesus because unlike commercials that claim their products will make your life better, Jesus really will!

STEP 2 MOVING UP

This step helps students learn that the best way to share with nonbelievers about Christ is through the way they live their lives.

Option 1 Move It

You'll need Several Bibles, six or seven objects that would be hard to identify without light, including a jar of unsalted peanuts and an identical jar of salted peanuts and a dark bag in which to put the objects.

Ahead of time, think of something on each object for students to identify. For example, if one of your objects is a book, the students could be asked to read the title or if one of your objects is an apple, the students could be asked to identify the color. The idea is to ask something that can't be answered without seeing the object in the light. Place the objects in the bag and keep it closed until the game.

Divide students into two teams. Call one team "salt" and the other "light." Have the teams move to the opposite end of the room from you and sit on the floor in their team groups. Tell them that you are going to have a contest to see which team can correctly identify something about the objects you will pull out of your bag. Explain that they'll need to tell you specifically what you will ask them about the object, whether it's the title, the color, the shape, etc. Turn off the lights in the room. Pull the objects out of the bag one by one. If a student thinks he can identify what you're holding, have him stand up and shout out the name of his team. Call on the first person you hear and ask for his answer. If he's correct say "That's right!" If he's incorrect say "That's wrong!" and don't reveal what the object really is. After the student has guessed, put the object in a place where it can be seen at the end of the game. When all the objects have been used, turn on the lights and let the students see the objects. Hopefully you'll have some funny mistakes to capitalize upon as you ask:

What made this game difficult? It was hard to see without light.

Have you ever searched for something in the dark? Keys, the doorknob of your house, the name on a street sign, etc.

What advantages are there to having light? We can see clearly.

Hand out a few unsalted peanuts to each student and instruct them to eat the peanuts. Next give them the salted peanuts to eat and ask: **What was the difference between these two peanuts? Which did you like more?** Explain: **It's amazing how a few grains of salt can make a big difference in the way something tastes.**

Transition: **Jesus told a story about salt and light.** Ask a volunteer to read Matthew 5:13-16. Explain: **Jesus used two images to help us understand what our lives as His followers should be like—salt and light. Let's talk about each of these symbols individually.**

Continue: **Just as we discovered in our game, things are a lot easier to see when there's light. The same holds true for us as well. People can see the Lord and His great love for them more clearly when we, as His people, are living out what we say we believe. Loving, godly lives are like beacons that direct people to Jesus. When we live out our faith in our words and actions we are being God's representatives and lighting the way for others to find a relationship with Him. When we don't live out our faith in what we do, it's like having a match, but never lighting it. Jesus has given us His light; what will we do with it?**

Conclude: **Even though our lives may seem small, just like the grains of salt on the peanuts, we can make a big impact on people around us. The salt in our lives is what we do to express our faith in God, such as kindness, patience, honesty, etc. When we live out our faith, others will notice that something is different about us. Then we can tell them why—Jesus has put His Spirit in us and changed us from the inside out!**

Option 2 Chat Room

You'll need Several Bibles.

Ahead of time, ask one of your most outgoing (and maybe even a bit obnoxious) students to prepare to act out the following wrong emotions: She should look very sad but yell, "I'm so happy!" Next, she should look absolutely terrified but moan, "I'm so sad!" Finally, she should act really angry but say, "This is such a terrific day!"

Begin: **Today we're going to look at a parable that Jesus told about salt and light.** Ask a volunteer to read Matthew 5:13-16. Once he has finished, ask a second student to read it again for emphasis. **Jesus used the images of salt and light to show that our lives should make a visible or obvious difference in the world around us. Just as we can taste the salt in our food or see the light in a room, we need to live out our faith in a way that makes it obvious who we are—disciples of Jesus. This only happens when we are living out in our actions what we say we believe in our hearts.**

Ask the volunteer to come to the front of the room and act out the three scenarios where the emotions don't match the words. Then ask: **What do all of these actions have in common?** The action didn't match the feeling.

Read James 2:14-17 to the students. Explain: **Just like it doesn't work when what we say doesn't match how we act, the same is true when we follow Jesus. If we say we follow Jesus, we should be salt to the bland world around us and a light to our friends who are trying to find the truth.** Discuss:

How are we supposed to let our lights shine before others? By living among people and letting them see Jesus in us.

What are specific ways that you let your light shine? Opening the door for someone, sharing your lunch, helping someone study, clearing the dinner dishes, volunteering at a day camp, going on a missions trip, etc. Anytime you touch others with God's love you are shining His light.

What suggestions would you have for someone who feels like he or she can't live out their faith? Remember that the Source of the light is Jesus. With His help we can show others that our faith is real. Being a light is not about proving something, it's about letting the inward change of heart come out naturally in the way you live your everyday life.

Who is the salt that loses its saltiness? People who say they believe in Jesus but do not live for Him.

What happens when we cover up a light? It becomes ineffective. People can no longer see their way.

Read Philippians 2:12-15 aloud, emphasizing verse 13; then ask: **How can we be sure that we are being salt and light?** To start with, have a consistent, daily devotional time with the Lord through prayer and reading His Word. Remember, it is God's work in us that enables us to live out our faith in Him.

Option 3 Pulse Points

You'll need Your Bible, a flashlight or battery-powered camping lantern, a small blanket, enough salted peanuts to give each student a handful, a blindfold, paper cups and enough water to give each student a drink.

The Big Idea
God wants us to live out our belief in Him.

The Big Question
How do we live out our belief in God?

Read Matthew 5:13-16. Explain: **Jesus is not just a part of life. He *is* life, and everything we are changes when we give our lives to Him. Those changes should be obvious to others. Jesus used two images—salt and light—to describe how our lives should affect those around us. Our lives, everything about us, should say "I belong to God."**

1. You are the light of the world.
Turn out the lights. Try to make the room as dark as possible. Turn on the flashlight or electric camping lantern and ask: **What is the purpose and benefit of having light in the darkness?** To guide those who don't have light to safety.

After students have responded, throw a blanket over the light. Ask: **Is the light doing its job now?** Read John 1:4 and explain: **Jesus put His life in us when we received His gift of salvation. That life brings light to us, changes us to be like Him and draws others to God. To have His light inside but not let it shine through our words and actions is like throwing a blanket over a light. Our outward life must reflect the inward light of Christ.**

2. You are the salt of the earth.
Ask for a volunteer to come forward for a quick taste test. Blindfold the volunteer and ask him to open his mouth. Place one salted peanut in his mouth and ask: **What are you eating?** Hopefully the volunteer will say "A peanut." **What flavor did you notice first?** Hopefully the response will be "Salt." Explain: **Salt makes things tasty. It is an obvious seasoning that is easily detected.**

Bible Bonus Note

Jesus' use of salt in this passage made sense to His listeners because salt was highly valued in Jesus' day. The Greeks called salt "divine." When Jesus used this analogy, He was connecting in these ways:

Salt was connected with purity. The Romans believed that salt was the purest of all things because it came from the purest of all places—the sun and the sea. At the end of the day, Jewish sacrifices were offered with salt.

Salt was a preservative. In Jesus' day salt was used to keep food from going bad and was even used to keep decay from getting worse. Jesus wants His hearers to understand that the Christian's influence in the world should prevent corruption and decay.

Salt was used to flavor food. From biblical times until now, salt has been used to season food, either during cooking or while being eaten. Jesus wants us to understand that a Christian should bring life and vitality to the world around him or her.

Salt was also used for healing. In the Old Testament, newborn babies were bathed and salted (Ezekiel 16:4), and in some cultures, they still are. Jesus knew that His listeners would know this and would thus realize that God wanted to use them to bring healing to situations around them. (Adapted from *The Gospel of Matthew, Volume 1* by William Barclay [Philadelphia: The Westminster Press, 1958], pp. 114-116.)

Give each student a handful of salted peanuts to eat as you read out loud again Matthew 5:13-16. Once they have finished explain: **Salt changes the flavor of food. Even a pinch can make an otherwise bland meal taste great. Our lives can seem too small to make a significant impact on the world around us. Yet a little can go a long way! Every time we show kindness, joy, peace, servanthood, generosity, etc., we are letting a few grains of salt shake out of our lives and change the flavor of the world around us.**

Continue: **Being a disciple of Jesus should be a joyful relationship that causes others to want what we have.** By now the students should be getting thirsty from the salt they just ate. (If not, keep talking until they will admit that they need something to drink!) Ask if anyone is thirsty. Sum up: **If someone gets enough salt, she will look for water. If someone sees us living out our faith she will get thirsty for the Living Water that comes from God.** Give students a drink of water before you go on.

STEP 3 — MOVING ON

This step helps students brainstorm ways their own lives can be like salt and light for their friends.

Option 1 — Chat Room

You'll need A Bible, white board, a dry-erase marker (or chalkboard and chalk) and copies of "Tough Calls" (p. 63).

Have students form pairs and give each pair a copy of "Tough Calls." Ask each pair to prepare a role play using their assigned situation. Allow a few minutes to create the role plays, encouraging them to be creative as they work through their situations.

After they've created their role plays, ask for a few pairs to present them in front of the class. After each role play ask the audience to suggest other ways to be salt and light.

Once this is done, ask volunteers to share a time when they've tried to tell their friends about Christ, but have felt like failures. Read Matthew 28:16-20. Ask: **How can you** apply this verse to the times when you feel like you've been rejected for trying to be different from others? We can know that Jesus is always with us, which empowers us to keep sharing, even if people at first reject our salt and light. Ask students to brainstorm 10 ways they can be like salt and light to people around them this week and write those 10 ideas on the board.

Option 2 — Real Life

You'll need Two copies of "Girls in Action" (p. 64), a white board and a dry-erase marker (or chalkboard and chalk).

Ahead of time, choose two of your most self-confident junior high girls to memorize and practice the drama.

Have the two girls present the "Girls in Action" drama. After they have finished, explain that although it seemed like Felicia was on the right track, what Jeannette needed was someone to just listen to her, help her with her homework and come to her birthday party. Telling others about Jesus is important, but sometimes we need to earn the right to be heard first—by showing God's love through our words, attitudes and actions.

Ask: **What are some ways we can earn the right to be heard this week at school? How does this relate to being salt and light?** Often earning the right to be heard means we have to be bold and different from the people around us, making us salt and light. Felicia would have been a huge light to Jeannette if she had truly befriended her, come to her birthday party and helped her with her homework.

Ask students to brainstorm ten ways they can be good and salty to people around them this week and write those ten ideas on the board.

Option 3 — Tough Questions

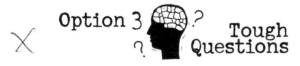

You'll need Time to review these questions before discussing them with the group.

1. **Why do we need to tell people about Jesus? Since God already has a plan for the world, why can't He just save people without using us?** God does have a plan for the world, but He's chosen to use us in telling people about Him. God modeled for us how He worked through His Son while He was a human, and

He still works through humans 2,000 years later. Also, using us to tell people about Jesus helps us to learn more about Him and teaches us to trust Him.

2. **Since some people have the gift of evangelism, why does everyone have to be salt and light? Why can't we each do our own thing (exercise our own gift) for the Lord and let evangelists bring people to Jesus?** Everyone has a different spiritual gift, but there is no passage in the Bible that says that only certain people should tell others about Christ. In Matthew 28:18-20, Jesus told *all* of the disciples to "go and make disciples." We all have a responsibility to tell others.

3. **What happens when we sin in front of unbelievers? Does that mean that our witness among unbelieving people is ruined?** We're imperfect people. We will make mistakes. It's important that we remember to ask for God's forgiveness when we do sin. If we ruin our witness in front of people, it's always best to ask their forgiveness. Doing this might also be a great witness.

STEP 4 — MOVING OUT

This step allows students to repent of one thing in their lives that keeps them from being His salt and light.

Option 1 — Light the Fire

You'll need A garbage can with some stinky trash in it, paper and pens or pencils.

Explain: **Living a life that is salt and light to others means we have to get rid of anything that makes our salty flavor bland or dulls our light.** Pick up a piece of trash and continue: **Anything that keeps us from being a light for God is like this piece of trash—stinky and no good.**

Ask students to think about one thing in their lives that is blocking their light from others and have them write it down on a piece of paper. When they have finished, ask them to come put their piece of paper in the trash with the rest of the garbage.

When everyone has finished, collect the trash and if there's a dumpster nearby, walk the entire class to the dumpster and watch all of the things that block their light go into the trash. Close in prayer, asking God to help us continue to remove anything that dulls our ability to be salt and light.

Option 2 — Fired Up

You'll need A container in which to burn paper (like a large metal trash can or a barbecue), sheets of paper, matches, pens or pencils and a small salt packet for each student (these can be found at a restaurant supply store or your local fast food restaurant).

> **CAUTION**
> This activity needs to be done outside or you need to take extra precautions to avoid setting off fire alarms or burning down the building!

Explain: **God's call to Christians to live a life before nonbelieving people is a high and holy call. Think about it; you have the opportunity to introduce people to the One who created oceans, capillaries and bugs. And even better, you have the chance to give others the opportunity to live forever. We must not take this opportunity lightly. God's call is also all-consuming. That means He wants us to get rid of whatever is holding us back from living so others will see Jesus.**

Ask students to think about the way they live. Help them understand that this activity isn't an attempt to push them into changing their lives because of guilt, but a chance to choose to live differently so others will see God in them. Distribute paper and pens or pencils. Instruct students to write the things on this paper that they need to sacrifice in order to live their lives so that others will see Jesus. You might need to give them some guidance as to what those things might be.

When students have finished thinking and writing, light a few papers on fire to get things started. Then invite students to come forward as they feel led and drop their papers in the fire. Instruct them to pray and ask God to help them live a life that is truly salt and light as their

papers burn. As students leave, give each one a small salt packet as a reminder to live a "salty" life.

Option 3 — Spread the Fire

You'll need A TV, a VCR, a video camera, a blank videotape and one small salt packet for each student (these can be found at a restaurant supply store or your local fast food restaurant).

Ahead of time, go to a nearby junior high campus and videotape various locations such as the lunch area, a classroom or two, the bike racks and the parking lot. **Suggestion:** If you have students from various schools attending the youth group, it would be a good idea to videotape a few locations from each of the schools students attend.

Explain: **We have so many opportunities around us to be salt and light and yet sometimes we don't realize it.** Play the videotape of the school, using the pause feature on the VCR at each new location so that the picture remains on the screen for approximately 20 seconds as you ask students to call out ways they could be salt and light in that location.

Ask students to find a partner and share one sin or obstacle that is getting in the way of their chances to be salt and light in their school. Have the partners pray for one another, confessing their sins to God and realizing that His forgiveness is available to them. Encourage them to exchange phone numbers or E-mail addresses and to contact each other during the week to see how they're doing at staying away from these sins. As students leave, give each one a small salt packet as a reminder to live a "salty" life.

Note
1. Wayne Rice, "The Diamond Merchant" *Hot Illustrations for Youth Talks* (Grand Rapids, MI: Zondervan Publishing House, 1994), pp. 83, 84.

Tough Calls

Tough Call One

You've been friends with Dylan for about three months. He's been honest with you about everything—including his belief that Christianity is fake and useless. You, however, have been faithful in attending church and going to youth group all your life.

One day you really blow it. First, Dylan sees you and your mom in a huge argument. Then you get ticked off with another friend and tell him off. You're having a bad day and Dylan takes this opportunity to ask you what the difference is between your beliefs and his. "After all," he says, "you have the same problems I do. Isn't life supposed to be better for you?"

What will you say? How will you share your faith in Jesus?

Tough Call Two

You've been trying to live for Jesus, but sometimes it can be so hard. It's especially difficult to live for Him around your parents. You accepted Christ last summer at camp, but your parents still don't understand what the big deal is. In fact, they've been openly hostile toward your beliefs. But you want to tell them more about Jesus and your desire to live for Him.

It's Friday night and you're watching television in the den. Your mom comes in and notices that the show you're watching uses some questionable language. Not really bad, but questionable. Just as one actor cuts loose with another creative swearword, you look up and notice your mom frowning at you.

At this moment you wonder if what you are watching on television is consistent with what you've told your parents about your beliefs.

What will you say? What will you do?

Tough Call Three

You've been dating Betsy for the last six months. You really like her and the two of you have an awesome time together, but you've never spoken with her about your beliefs, and lately you feel like you need to.

You've asked Betsy to eat lunch with you to have a long talk. She's not sure what to expect, but loves a free lunch and loves being with you. So with Betsy sitting across the table from you, you begin to tell her about your belief in God. What will you say?

GIRLS IN ACTION

Cast

Jeannette, a Christian
Felicia, a non-Christian

The scene opens with Felicia sitting in a chair, as if at a table in a coffee shop; Jeannette walks in.

Felicia: Hey, Jeannette, what's up?

Jeannette: Hey, Felicia, I haven't seen you in a while. I missed you at my birthday party last week.

Felicia: Yeah, sorry, I just got really busy.

Jeannette: Well, anyway, I'm glad you're here. I'm so upset.

Felicia: Why? What's going on?

Jeannette: Well, since you stopped helping me with math, I've been bombing. I tried to hide my report card from my mom, but she found it in my desk and she is totally ticked. She said that I can't spend any more time with friends after school until my grades get better.

Felicia: That stinks.

Jeannette: I know, doesn't it? She's at the grocery store now, so I kinda snuck out. She doesn't know I'm here.

Felicia: (Hesitating.) Well, Jeannette, maybe now is a good time to tell you about a friend of mine.

Jeannette: Yeah, I know, you think that I'm too mean to that new girl, Tammy.

Felicia: No, actually, I mean my friend Jesus. He's my best friend in the whole world. And even though you can't see any other friends right now, you could ask Him to come into your life and be your Savior.

Jeannette: Look, Felicia, I don't want to hear about Jesus right now. I need someone who is here right now to help me, and here you go telling about some guy who died a long time ago. I need a friend I can see, that I can count on to be there for me! If you were really a friend, you would have come to my birthday party and you would have helped me with my homework.

(Jeannette walks off the stage angrily.)

Devotions in Motion

WEEK FOUR: LIVING OUR FAITH:
SALT AND LIGHT

DAY 1

Quick Questions

Jump into 1 Timothy 2:3,4 and see what God wants saved: pennies? bottle caps? gum wrappers?

God Says

Did you ever join a club when you were a kid? What was it about?

To become a club member did you have to do things like jump into a river or pull a prank on someone?

Does being a Christian mean being in a club where you have to do things such as dressing right or paying your dues?

God's gift of salvation is not a like a club membership where only a few get to join. He wants everyone to be saved! And being saved is not about following rules or paying your dues. It is a completely new way of living—a total change in heart and lifestyle. When we let that new life shine through us, others will see the way to God.

I Do

What would Jesus say about your life as this follower? Is there a way to let this light shine even brighter in you this week?

Pray for God to use you to draw someone closer to Himself.

FOLD HERE ---

DAY 4

Fast Facts

Find Matthew 28:16-20 and see what Jesus saved for last.

God Says

Mark went to live with his Dad for the summer, on the other side of the country far away from his mom. His mom sent him a long letter after he had been gone only a few days. She told him how his little sister and grandmother were and how things were going with her job. She told him how the weather was and told him a joke she thought he would like.

At the very end of the letter she wrote, "Be good. Make sure you take good care of yourself. Eat good food and sleep enough at night. I love you and miss you." She saved the most important things for last.

I Do

Jesus thought that sharing the good news with everyone was really important. He made it one of the last things He said to us so that we would remember it.

Ask God to show you ways to do what He asked all week.

Fast Facts

Feeling bold? Find Acts 5:27-29 and learn what God means by the word "bold."

God Says

David felt sort of weird about being a Christian. He went to a public school and took his Bible to school every day, but no one ever gave him a hard time about it. All his non-Christian friends knew he went to church and none of them stopped being his friend because of it.

One weekend he went to church and the pastor spoke about how important it was to tell your friends about God and to be bold. On Monday, David went to school knowing that it wasn't enough just to take his Bible in his backpack to school with him and let his friends know he went to church. He needed to be more bold and actually tell his friends about Jesus.

I Do

David could lose his friends by being more bold. Is it worth it? If you think so, pray that God will help you be bold with your friends, with your family and with the people you meet each day.

FOLD HERE ---

Quick Questions

Flip, flip, flip to Matthew 4:18-19 and find out what complicated things God needs from you?

God Says

If you were going fishing, what would you need to take with you?

- ☐ Books about calculus, nuclear physics and pond life
- ☐ A guy named Floyd with his Ph.D. in fishing
- ☐ Fishing poles made of titanium lures made of pure gold
- ☐ A boat made of glass

I Do

Fishing is a simple thing that doesn't require lots of fancy stuff. How is that like showing people the truth?

Jesus told His followers to simply, "Come." Do you think God wants it to be complicated or simple when you share the truth with the people you know?

Who is one person you can share the truth with this week?

The Big Idea

Forgiveness is always the right choice.

Session Aims

In this session you will guide students to:

- Learn that forgiving others makes sense because God forgives us;
- Understand the importance of making forgiving others a daily practice;
- Commit to choosing one person to forgive, even though it may be tough.

The Biggest Verse

"Then the master called the servant in. 'You wicked servant,' he said, 'I canceled all that debt of yours because you begged me to. Shouldn't you have had mercy on your fellow servant just as I had on you?'" Matthew 18:32,33

Other Important Verses

Amos 1:3,6,9,11,13; 2:1,4,6; Matthew 6:14; 18:21-35; Romans 12:18; Ephesians 4:32; Colossians 3:13; 1 Peter 3:9

Forgiveness: The Unforgiving Servant

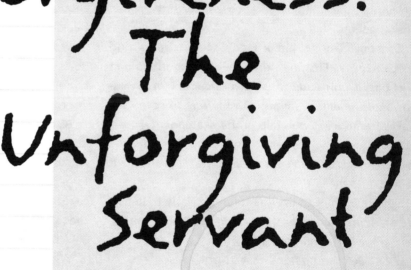

STEP

MOVING IN

This step gets students thinking about how rarely we forgive other people.

Option 1 — Move It

You'll need One white bedsheet or large piece of white paper, one clear plastic tarp, ketchup, mustard, grape jelly, barbecue sauce and any other colorful liquids (at least five different colors) you can find, paper towels and a trash can or trash bag.

Ahead of time, lay the clear plastic tarp over the white sheet (or paper) on the floor in the center of the room.

As students arrive, welcome them and explain: **We're going to start today by taking a look at 24 hours in the life of a typical junior higher whom we'll call "Junior."** Explain that the white bedsheet covered with the plastic tarp represents "Junior."

Continue: **During Junior's day several interesting things happen. First, he's grumpy in the morning and talks back to his dad.** At this point pour one of the liquids onto the tarp. Continue: **On his way to school he makes fun of a kid who falls off his skateboard.** Pour a second liquid onto the tarp. Continue naming sins and pouring liquids until you have at least five different liquids poured onto the tarp.

Explain: **Each of us lives each day similarly to Junior. We do dumb, hurtful or sinful things and make a mess.** Mix up the liquids and continue: **There's only one thing that can clean us up—and that's forgiveness.**

Discuss:

What does it mean to be forgiven? It means that whatever we've done wrong is forgotten.

What does the world say forgiveness is? Forgiving, but not forgetting.

Why is it important that we forgive others? Because Jesus tells us to. Plus if we don't, we can cause ourselves emotional damage and put a wall between ourselves and others and between ourselves and God.

Transition to a deeper level by asking: **What does God's forgiveness do?** It washes away our sin and allows us to enter heaven.

At this point carefully lift the clear covering with the gross liquids off Junior as you continue: **Forgiveness is the only thing that can get rid of all the wrong things you and I do every day.** Carefully roll up the tarp and discard it in a trash can or trash bag.

Explain: **Today we'll be talking about the importance of forgiving others. We'll look at what Jesus says about it and figure out how what He says makes a difference in our own lives.**

Option 2 — Chat Room

You'll need Newspapers, a large sheet of newsprint (or a white board, chalkboard or overhead projector and transparencies), appropriate writing instruments and masking or transparent tape.

Ahead of time, gather several days' worth of newspapers, especially national newspapers with a wide variety of stories. Read through the newspapers and collect stories about people who have done terrible things such as committing murder, theft or arson. Make sure that you have enough of these for each pair to have one story. Depending on the size of your group and the amount of news in your city, to make sure that each student sees a news story, you may need to make several copies of three or four stories or modify the instructions below from "pairs" to "groups" of three to five students.

Also ahead of time, tape the large sheet of paper to a wall.

As students are arriving, welcome them and have them form pairs. Give each pair a news story. Instruct the pairs to read the story and be prepared to report the answers to the following questions:

What was the crime?
What was the criminal's attitude?
What was the punishment?

Give pairs a minute or two to prepare their answers. As groups are preparing their answers, write the three questions on the sheet of paper. When groups are ready, ask them to report their findings to the rest of the class. As they report, write their responses in the appropriate places on the newsprint (or board or overhead).

When all groups have responded, discuss:

What do you notice about punishment?

What do you notice about the criminals' attitudes?

If you had been the object of these crimes, would you be able to forgive these people? How? Why?

What is the difference between our forgiveness and God's?

Explain: **Today, we'll be talking about the difference between God's forgiveness and ours.**

Option 3  Fun and Games

You'll need One squirt gun with water in it for each student, one sheet of paper and masking tape. For each section of the room you'll need large amounts of individually wrapped candies. (Yum, yum, yum. If you have leftovers, you can mail them to the author!)

> **Note:** If it is not financially feasible to get a squirt gun for each student, modify the game below so that the students who receive squirt guns are the "defenders" while those without are the "attackers" who try to take the other teams' candy.

As students arrive, welcome them and divide them into teams of approximately 10 students each. Give each student a squirt gun, a piece of paper and a piece of masking tape. Each person should have the paper taped to his or her back. Divide the candy evenly between the teams and explain: **I'm going to assign each team to a territory of the room. Your job is to protect that territory and your candy without letting your paper get hit with water. I'll award the most points to the group that has the least amount of water on their papers when we all run out of water in our squirt guns.**

Assign each group a part of the room and some candy to protect. Explain that they must protect their candy while trying to sneak over to other groups' areas and try to take the other teams' candy. The game is over when everyone's squirt gun is empty.

Give the teams a minute to prepare and figure out their strategy; then begin the game. When the game is over, be sure that everyone gets some candy; then discuss:

How difficult was it to keep from getting hit with water?

Why was it so hard?

Which was hardest, trying not to get hit or trying to get the candy? Why?

Explain: **Often when someone gets in our way, such as blocking us from the candy, or when someone hurts us, such as stepping on our foot or calling us a name, it's easy to get angry or frustrated. Yet Jesus has something else He'd like us to do. By the end of this meeting we're all going to walk out of this room with a better understanding of what Jesus would want us to do when someone hurts us.**

Youth Leader Tip

When working with junior high students, remember these cardinal rules:

Expect the unexpected. Young teens will always do the unexpected. Chalk it up to the clash between raging hormones and experimenting with different personalities. Be flexible. Laugh at the little things. When things don't go the way they're supposed to go (like what might happen with this rowdy game), get in on the action.

Go with the flow. Every discussion might not take the nicely plowed direction that you have planned. Be willing to leave the lesson for a bit (or trash it altogether) for the sake of going where students need to go.

Be a scholarly blockhead. The group you are teaching will contain students who know a lot, as well as students who know only a little about the teachings of Jesus. You need to be prepared to communicate some general truths with some simple and concrete illustrations. But at the same time, you've also got to be ready to ask deeper and more difficult questions to challenge junior highers' growing minds.

STEP 2 — MOVING UP

This step helps students learn that forgiving others makes sense because of the way God forgives us.

Option 1 — Move It

You'll need Several Bibles, masking tape, a stack of light green paper, a source of rowdy music and a $20 bill that you don't mind giving away. (If $20 is a little steep, $10 or even $5 will also make the point.)

Ahead of time, tape a line down the center of the floor of the meeting room to separate the two teams.

Divide students into two teams and explain that they're going to compete in a paper fight. You're going to throw out clumps of green paper and students should crumple them up and throw them to the other side of the room. Play a little rowdy music and then let the green paper go flying!

Just before you are ready to end the game, take the $20 bill, wad it into a green piece of paper and throw it into the game. End the game, congratulate the winner, and explain that you have a surprise: **There's a $20** (or $10 or $5) **bill hidden in one of these pieces of paper and whoever finds it gets to keep it.**

Once a student finds the $20 bill, explain: **Now I want you to imagine that I had only loaned you the $20 bill instead of giving it to you. Let's say you can't pay it back because you've been spending all your money on computer games. Since I'm a nice person, I decide to let you off the hook. The next day you see someone in the hallway at school who owes you a quarter, and you ask her for it. She says that she can't give it to you today, but maybe sometime next month. You are so angry that you yell at her in front of her friends. Do you think this is fair? Why?**

Explain that Jesus tells a similar story in Matthew 18:21-35. Ask for a volunteer to read the passage aloud; then discuss:

Who does the king represent? God.

Who does the servant represent? Us.

What is the significance of the difference in the size of the debts? The larger debt is our sin; the smaller debt is what others owe us.

What is the significance of the king canceling the servant's debt? This is a demonstration of God's forgiveness.

Why did the servant treat his fellow servant harshly? Because he didn't understand forgiveness and he was taking the king's forgiveness for granted.

What does Jesus want us to learn from this parable? Jesus wants us to forgive others in the same way that we've been forgiven. He wants us to understand that our debt to Him is far greater than anyone's debt to us, yet He forgives us completely!

Explain: **While we all might have different perspectives on what Jesus said, the truth is that He has called us to forgive others. It doesn't matter what others have done to us; forgiveness is always the right thing to do.**

Option 2  Chat Room

You'll need Several Bibles, two adult volunteers, one copy of "Forgiveness Perspectives" (p. 77) cut into three sections, paper and pens or pencils.

Ahead of time, ask one of the adult volunteers to come to you at the start of class and tell you in front of the students, "Hey, I know you owe me $20, but don't worry about it. Just call it a gift from me." Ask the other adult to play along with you when you belligerently ask him for the dollar that he owes you so that you can go get a soda.

As you begin this step, cue the first adult volunteer to mention your $20 debt. Begin telling a story about something that happened to you this week; then say to the second adult volunteer: **I hate to interrupt but I am *so* thirsty. Remember, you owe me a dollar? Can I have it now so I can go get a soda right after the meeting?** At this point the adult who allegedly owes you a dollar should explain that she didn't have time to go to the bank, so she's going to have to pay you later. You should get really mad at her and if you think you can pull it off, storm out of the room saying something like: **Fine, I'll just figure out how to get a drink myself!**

This will undoubtedly freak out students—which is exactly what you want to do. The surprise will make this step all the more memorable and powerful. Come back into the room and ask students what they were thinking as you got angry at the adult who owed you one dollar. Comment on how ironic and ludicrous this is since you were just forgiven a debt of $20.

Explain that Jesus told a similar story; then ask a volunteer to read Matthew 18:21-35 aloud. Discuss:

What are some of the similarities between what happened today and this story that Jesus tells?

Who does the king represent? God.

Who does the servant represent? Us.

What is the significance between the difference in the size of the debts? The larger the debt of our sin, the smaller the debt of what others owe us.

What is the significance of the king canceling the servant's debt? Jesus is showing us an awesome picture of His forgiveness.

Why does the servant treat his fellow servant harshly? Because he doesn't understand what forgiveness is and because he's greedy.

What does Jesus want us to learn from this parable? That forgiving others is something we must do. Jesus wants us to forgive others in the same way that we've been forgiven. He wants us to understand that our debt to Him is far greater than anyone's debt to us, yet He forgives us completely!

Explain that Jesus communicated the importance of forgiveness. He pointed out that since we've been forgiven so much, we should forgive others. Help students understand that in Jewish law, forgiving others three times was normal (see Bible Bonus Note p. 72). But Jesus makes the point that we are supposed to constantly forgive others. Jesus' use of "seventy times seven" was tongue-in-cheek. He doesn't want us just to multiply those numbers (490, by the way) and only forgive someone that many times; He wants us to see that we need to forgive an indefinite number of times.

Divide students into three groups. Give each group one of the "Forgiveness Perspectives" cards. Instruct them to read their assigned perspective and answer the questions from that perspective. Allow groups five minutes to read the passage and write their answers. When groups are finished, have them share their reactions with the whole group.

NOTES

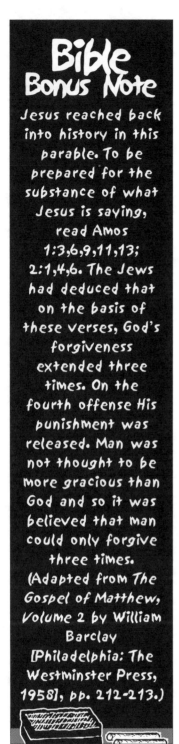

Bible Bonus Note

Jesus reached back into history in this parable. To be prepared for the substance of what Jesus is saying, read Amos 1:3,6,9,11,13; 2:1,4,6. The Jews had deduced that on the basis of these verses, God's forgiveness extended three times. On the fourth offense His punishment was released. Man was not thought to be more gracious than God and so it was believed that man could only forgive three times. (Adapted from *The Gospel of Matthew, Volume 2* by William Barclay [Philadelphia: The Westminster Press, 1958], pp. 212-213.)

Option 3  Pulse Points

You'll need Several Bibles, sticky notes, felt-tip pens, masking tape and one large sheet of paper (large enough to wrap around someone) with the words "Personal Pain" written on it.

The Big Idea

Our forgiveness of others flows out of God's forgiveness for us.

The Big Question

How does God's forgiveness of us relate to our forgiveness of others?

Forgiving others is essential—though not always easy. Use this activity to help students understand how to forgive.

Ask for a volunteer to come forward who doesn't mind being covered with a large sheet of paper for the next few minutes; then distribute one sticky note and a felt-tip pen to each student. (If you don't have enough pens for each student to have one, ask them to share.)

Have students write one sin that they've committed—something they have done that is not what God would want them to do. Encourage them to write only what they feel comfortable with other students knowing. As students are writing their sins, wrap the volunteer with the large sheet of paper. When students are finished writing, have them place their notes on their chests.

Begin: **Forgiveness is an unusual thing. The world wants us to think that holding grudges is okay. But Jesus makes it clear that forgiveness is always the best option.** Help them understand this by reading Matthew 18:21-35. Then help them understand the two sides of forgiveness by sharing the following points.

1. God forgives us.

Explain: **The first and most important side of forgiveness is that God forgives us of all the wrong things we have done. That's important because without God's forgiveness, we'd be eternally lost.** Point out to students the sticky notes they have attached to their chests. Help them understand that without God's forgiveness we'd walk around forever branded by our sin, but because of God's forgiveness, we can walk around free. Have students take off their notes and wad them up.

Explain: **Even though we've been forgiven of terrible things, sometimes we refuse to show others the same grace, which is the next point in this outline.** (How convenient, huh?)

2. We forgive others.

Explain: **The second side of forgiveness is forgiving others.** Point out the volunteer you have wrapped in the paper. Continue: **When we choose not to forgive people, we're not obeying God, which hurts us and our relationship with Him. But we also hurt the person we choose not to forgive because he may feel trapped in personal pain, just as the student is trapped in the paper right now.** Have students hurl their crumpled-up sins at the person.

Explain: **Forgiving others not only frees us, it frees the people we forgive.** Rip the paper off the volunteer as a symbol of this fact. Continue: **The words that Jesus spoke to the disciples about this were remarkable. They were looking for an exact legal definition for how to live. They were looking for a specific number of times. Jesus' command was not to stick to a specific number times of forgiveness, but to live a life of forgiveness.**

STEP 3 — MOVING ON

This step helps students understand how they can make forgiving others a daily practice.

Option 1 — Chat Room

You'll need Several Bibles and an adult volunteer.

Ahead of time, ask one of the adult volunteers, a student or someone else in your church to come prepared to give a brief testimony about one specific way someone has hurt them and how they are learning—or have already learned—to forgive that person. Ask the person sharing the testimony to share authentically and vulnerably about the pain he or she has experienced, how difficult it can be to forgive someone, and how freeing it is to forgive. Warn the volunteer to be careful not to use names or details that would give hints to the identity of the forgiven person.

Begin: **Forgiving others can be such a hard thing to do. I've invited someone to tell us more about how he (or she) has been learning about forgiveness firsthand.** Invite the person you've prepared in advance to give his or her testimony. Then discuss the following with the whole group:

Why is forgiving others so difficult? Because we are human and we feel things deeply. When we're wronged, it takes a lot of work to forgive.

What happens if we choose not to forgive people? Ultimately, we aren't doing what Jesus asks us to do.

Is there anything someone can to do us that is not forgivable? Nope, especially when we remember all the "stuff" God forgives us for!

Explain: **God reminds us of His forgiveness so that we'll mirror His actions. God wants us to forgive like He does.** Read Ephesians 4:32 and 1 Peter 3:9 to help students understand this fact.

Help students also understand that God doesn't expect us to blindly forgive everyone who wrongs us. We should always hope that others will ask for our forgiveness. But God doesn't make that a condition of our forgiveness. He asks us to forgive no matter what, who, when or where.

Option 2 — Real Life

You'll need Several Bibles.

Gather students in the center of the room and read this case study to them. Then discuss the questions that follow:

Jim always wanted a job at the fitness club. Ever since he could remember, working at the club was what he hoped to do when he turned 16. He loved working out. He loved talking about working out. He loved playing racquetball and swimming with his friends at the club. Through the years he'd maintained a great friendship with the owner. Often when things were slow at the club, he and the owner, Bob, would see who could bench press the most. Jim would always lose, but he didn't care. Just being with Bob made it worthwhile. Bob had promised to hire Jim when he was old enough.

Every birthday was one year closer to his dream. Every year Jim looked forward to the day when Bob would hire him. Jim didn't want to run the place. He didn't even want to move up in the fitness world. He just wanted to work at the club. It meant everything to him.

Jim was ecstatic when his sixteenth birthday came. His parents got him an old used car. "Great!" Jim thought to himself, "I can use this to get back and forth from the club. And the money I make there will certainly be enough to pay for the gas!"

His birthday was on a Sunday and the club was closed. So on Monday he went down after school to talk to Bob about the job he had promised Jim. Jim bounced into Bob's office singing "Happy Birthday" as a little hint of why he was there.

"Hi, Jim. What's up?"

"*Well*, I'm 16 now. And you promised me that when I turned 16 you would hire me. So here I am! When do I start?"

"Oh! Well, you see Jim, it's like this. I like hanging out with you. You're a great kid. But I don't think you've got what it takes to work here. I really don't need anyone to work afternoons and evenings. And all my talk about giving you a job? I was just kidding with you. I thought you understood."

Jim flew into a rage. He shoved Bob and slammed the office door. And as he stomped to his car, he said some things that he wished he hadn't.

And now, even though working at the club was what he had always wanted, it was the last place he ever wanted to be.

Discuss:

What did Bob do wrong?

Was Jim's reaction appropriate?

Should Jim forgive Bob? Why?

Should Bob forgive Jim for losing control?

Why is forgiving others so difficult? Because we are human and we feel things deeply. When we're wronged, it takes a lot of work to forgive.

What's the best way to handle ourselves when we need to forgive someone? Take time to think. Ask for reasons why the hurt happened. Seek out someone you can trust to talk to about your hurt.

Divide students into four groups. Assign each group one of the following passages: Matthew 6:14; Ephesians 4:32; Colossians 3:13; 1 Peter 3:9. Have groups read their assigned verse; then have group members share about a time when they had difficulty forgiving someone and how their assigned verse relates to their need to forgive others.

Close by explaining: **God reminds us of His forgiveness so that we'll mirror His actions. Even though forgiving others feels like it might be impossible, His grace and strength can help us do it.**

NOTES

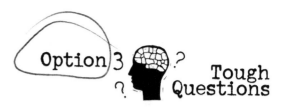

Option 3 — Tough Questions

You'll need Several Bibles and these questions.

1. **Even though God forgives us, why should we forgive others? Isn't forgiving others God's business?** Yes and no. Ultimately, forgiveness comes from God. But in order to live at peace with people and our selves and do what Jesus says, we must forgive people who wrong us.

2. **What do you do if you're in a fight with a friend and think it's 10 percent your fault and 90 percent his fault?** Well, first of all you may be responsible for more than you think. But regardless, the biblical principles that we've learned about still apply. You can ask forgiveness for the part of the fight that you think is your fault and even if your friend doesn't ask forgiveness for what is his "fault," you need to forgive him because of how much Jesus has forgiven you.

3. **Why shouldn't we wait for someone to ask us for forgiveness before we forgive him or her?** That's great if it happens, but it doesn't always work that way. We need to forgive people whether or not they ever ask us to or to say they're sorry.

4. **What if someone keeps hurting you? Do you ever stop forgiving them?** The scriptural principles of forgiveness from this session apply whether it's the first time they've hurt us or the billionth time they've hurt us. But if you notice a pattern that isn't changing, you should try to talk to that person, and if he or she doesn't change, you should prayerfully consider staying away from him or her as much as possible.

The Bible says much more about forgiving others: Matthew 6:14; Romans 12:18; Ephesians 4:32; Colossians 3:13; 1 Peter 3:9. Have volunteers read the verses and ask students to comment on what these verses say about forgiving others.

STEP 4 MOVING OUT

This step challenges students to each choose one person to forgive.

Option 1  Light the Fire

You'll need 3x5-inch index cards, pens or pencils, transparent tape and a cross—either a large wooden one, a cardboard cutout or one drawn on a large sheet of paper and taped to the wall.

Explain: **God's desire for us to forgive people is essential for a number of reasons. First, we must forgive people because He asks us to. Second, we must forgive people because it's the best way to have relationships with others. And finally, God wants us to forgive people because He knows that if we don't it might cause us permanent emotional pain which leads to bitterness.**

Ask students to close their eyes and continue: **We've all been wronged by someone. I'd like you to think about someone who did something to you that you might not have forgiven yet. If you need to forgive someone, now is the time to ask God for help in taking the first step.**

Distribute index cards and pens or pencils. Instruct students to write something that has happened to them that is hard to forgive. To ensure confidentiality, suggest that students just write the first letter of whatever happened to them such as writing *G* for gossiping about me or *L* for lying about me.

Allow two or three minutes for writing; then explain: **The best way to ask God for help is to lay our burdens at the Cross. When we do that, we are saying that we know we can't do it on our own, but we need Him to help us.** Have students tape their cards to the cross.

When everyone has taped their cards, have students gather in a circle around the cross and close with prayer asking God for help in forgiving others.

After students leave, be sure to completely destroy their notes to ensure confidentiality.

Option 2 Fired Up

You'll need Copies of "Forgiveness Certificate" (p. 78) and pens or pencils.

Explain: **God's call on our lives to forgive people is a lifestyle call. God isn't asking us to just forgive a few people; He is asking us to make forgiveness part of who we are. Sometimes that can be very difficult.** Tell students that you will give them an opportunity to make a commitment to choose to live a life of forgiveness.

Distribute "Forgiveness Certificate" and pens or pencils and as students are completing the handouts, explain: **Take a moment to look at your certificate. Consider what you are doing. You are telling God that you are willing to forgive people who wrong you no matter what, when or why. I'd like you to remember your commitments today, but I'd like you to leave your certificates here when you leave. I'll mail them to you later to remind you of your commitment.**

> **Note:** To save time, give the envelopes to students and ask them to address envelopes to themselves before leaving.

Be sure to mail students' certificates 30 days after this study to serve as a reminder of the commitments they've made.

Option 3  Spread the Fire

> This "Spread the Fire" option calls for real maturity, so if you think this is too advanced for your students, choose the more accessible "Light the Fire" or "Fired Up" options.

You'll need Paper, envelopes and pens or pencils.

Explain: **Our ability to forgive has an impact on our lives, but it has an equally powerful impact on others' lives as they see God at work in us.** Ask students to think about someone they need to forgive. Explain that you'd like them to write letters to people who might need their forgiveness. Suggest that students briefly mention in their letters that since they've been forgiven by God, they know they need to forgive others. Make sure in your instructions that you clarify that students shouldn't ask forgiveness but really end up blaming the person or making excuses for what they've done. Writing, "I'm really sorry I called you 'dumb' yesterday, but you did give a stupid answer in history class" isn't really an apology. It actually places the blame back on the forgivee. Also warn students that the people they're writing to might not respond to forgiveness immediately. It might take some time, but the important thing is that the students did the right thing and asked forgiveness.

Distribute the paper, envelopes and pens or pencils. Give students five minutes to write their letters. When everyone is finished, encourage them to actually mail their letters to the people who need to know they've been forgiven. Close the meeting by asking everyone to gather in a circle in the center of the room and pray together, asking God's help in forgiving others and in being forgiven by others.

NOTES

Forgiveness Perspectives

Take a journey through time and imagine you're this person, living in Jesus' time.

You're a Jewish person. Your father, your father's father and your father's father's father have believed in God and have left you with the wonderful heritage and history of Israel. All that heritage has caused you to trust in God as a righteous judge. You believe that God loves all people, but that when someone sins against Him, he/she deserves His wrath. Therefore you believe that once someone wrongs you more than three times, you should not forgive him/her. News has just reached you about what Jesus says about forgiveness. What are your reactions?

Take a journey through time and imagine you're this person, living in Jesus' time.

You're a Gentile. Well, at least that's what people call you—you really have no idea what you are, but you do know that your family history has been less than religious. Hey, you're not the most evil person in the world. You have broken a few of the laws that the Jews talk about, but it's not like you've murdered anyone. And you've never stolen either (unless that candy bar from the synagogue fund-raiser last year counts). You believe that God is real, but you haven't worked too hard at understanding His teachings. News has just reached you about what Jesus says about forgiveness. What are your reactions?

Take a journey through time and imagine you're this person, living in Jesus' time.

You're a murderer on the run. Last year in a fit of passion and rage, you killed a man for stealing the grain out of your storage shed. You aren't proud of what you did, but the grain that the man stole was supposed to feed your family and has left your kids without food. You aren't familiar with Jewish teachings, but you do know that murder is a pretty big deal. And because you don't want to get caught, you've uprooted your family, sold your home and have been on the move for the past six months. News has just reached you about what Jesus says about forgiveness. What are your reactions?

Forgiveness Certificate

I hereby promise to live a life of forgiveness. I plan on making it a daily practice to tell others that I forgive them. And I also promise not to hold a grudge against someone who has done something wrong to me.

_____ Signature
_____ Date
_____ Witness

"Bear with each other and forgive whatever grievances you may have against one another. Forgive as the Lord forgave you." Colossians 3:13

I hereby promise to live a life of forgiveness. I plan on making it a daily practice to tell others that I forgive them. And I also promise not to hold a grudge against someone who has done something wrong to me.

_____ Signature
_____ Date
_____ Witness

"Bear with each other and forgive whatever grievances you may have against one another. Forgive as the Lord forgave you." Colossians 3:13

Devotions in Motion

WEEK FIVE: FORGIVENESS: THE UNFORGIVING SERVANT

DAY 1

Fast Facts

Hey, don't go anywhere until you've read Matthew 18:21,22 and done a little math!

God Says

Andrew was so fed up with his little sister. While he was at school, she had gone into his room and into his drawers. She took a black marker and wrote all over the pages of his math book and she let his lizard, Elvis, out of his cage. This wasn't the first time either. She did things like this all the time! Only yesterday she had used his brand new toothbrush to do her Barbie's hair. When she came to apologize, Andrew said, "I have forgiven you a zillion times. I don't have to forgive you anymore!" Is that true?

I Do

Jesus didn't mean to give us a specific number when He told the disciples this. He wants us to keep on forgiving and forgiving and forgiving even when it seems like we've done it a million times. Ask God to help you forgive anyone who hurts you this week.

FOLD HERE -

DAY 4

Quick Questions

See if you can find Colossians 3:13,14 in under fifteen seconds!

God Says

How hard would it be to forgive...

☐ The most popular girl in school if she bumped into you and caused you to drop all your books and papers right in front of all her friends who all laughed at you?

☐ Your sister who ate the pizza you were saving for your snack after school when you were starved?

☐ The least popular guy in school if he spilled a milkshake on you just before you had to give an oral report in English?

I Do

Is it easier to practice forgiveness once in a while or every day?

Who is one person who has hurt you in the past that you should forgive?

Quick Questions

Discover Luke 11:2-4 and read an oldie but goodie.

God Says

How many times have you heard The Lord's Prayer? One million times? Or maybe just twice? Are the things in it easy to do?

How easy is it to forgive all the time?

Is it easy to forgive the most popular person in school if she does something mean to you?

What about the least popular person?

What about your siblings or your mom and dad?

Does God tell us to do these things because they are easy?

I Do.

Why does Jesus think forgiveness is so important?

Who is one person you need to forgive right now?

FOLD HERE --

Fast Facts

Flip to Luke 6:37,38 and you be the judge of whether or not you should be the judge.

God Says

Gina had more Bible awards than anyone had ever seen. She had 44 blue ribbons for memorizing Bible verses in elementary school, she had a pile of award Bibles that she never opened collecting dust in the corner of her closet, and she had two big gold trophies for winning The National Bible Verse Competition two years in a row. In spite of all these awards for knowing so much of The Bible, Gina was mean to others and acted like she was a better Christian than anyone who had ever lived before.

I Do.

Do you ever act like Gina?

Pray that God will get His Word from your ears to your brain and into your heart, helping you love and forgive everyone—just like God loves and forgives you!

SESSIONSIXSESSIONSIXSESSIONSIX

The Big Idea

Helping someone else is like helping Jesus.

Session Aims

In this session you will guide students to:

- Realize that serving others is like serving Jesus;
- Be encouraged to serve others even when the going gets tough;
- Choose one specific way they can serve their friends or family this week.

The Biggest Verse

"For I was hungry and you gave me something to eat, I was thirsty and you gave me something to drink, I was a stranger and you invited me in, I needed clothes and you clothed me, I was sick and you looked after me, I was in prison and you came to visit me." Matthew 25:35,36

Other Important Verses

Matthew 10:40-42; 25:31-46; John 3:16; 14:6; Ephesians 2:8,9; James 2:14-16; 1 Peter 4:11; 1 John 1:12-15

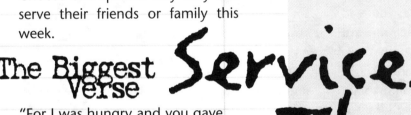

Service: The Sheep and Goats

STEP
MOVING IN

This step reminds students that serving others can be hard.

Option 1 Move It

You'll need Copies of "Pressure Stories" (p. 90).

Ahead of time, cut the copies of "Pressure Stories" apart, keeping the same stories together.

As students arrive, welcome and divide them into four equal groups. Explain: **I'm going to give each of you a card with a situation on it.** Continue explaining as you hand out one situation from "Pressure Stories" to each group: **I'd like you to remain totally silent as you read this story. Then I'd like each group to come forward one at a time and perform a skit in front of us that tells your assigned story in your own words and gives a possible ending for the story. There is one more thing: Each person may share only seven words per turn! For example, if your story is about someone who wants to serve by washing cars, it might go something like, "Bill wanted to serve others by washing..."** and then the next person might say, **"cars, so he headed out to get..."** and the next person would continue. **The story can't end until every student from your group has gone twice.** Give groups a few minutes to decide their ending; then have them perform their skit.

When groups are finished presenting, discuss:

What's the best way to serve others when we aren't sure how to do it?

What should we do when serving others is difficult?

Should we quit serving when we feel like it's too difficult?

Explain: **Sometimes serving others can feel like we're attempting a difficult task, but we're going to see today that God calls us to serve even when it gets tough or is not appreciated.**

Option 2 Chat Room

You'll need Just this book!

As students are arriving, welcome them. When everyone has arrived, instruct them to sit down. Read the following short story aloud:

Twenty years ago, long before Steve was born, his parents began attending a small church on the south side of the city. When they began attending the church it was the cool place to attend and the church was growing a lot. These days the church is in a difficult spot. Through the years, the neighborhood around the church has changed. Many of the people who attended the church moved to the north side of the city where there was a lot more grass, flowers, trees and really nice houses. Steve's family moved too. And even though they still attend the church on the south side, they were one of just a few families who stayed on.

Every week as they drove to church, Steve would notice the houses that surrounded the church. They were falling apart. There were cars with flat tires and missing parts parked out in front of these homes. One day Steve thought, *I wonder if God is calling me to serve these people?* **He figured that with their homes in the condition they were in, they would certainly welcome the help. So Steve decided he'd go around and offer to do free clean-up work at the homes that were around the church.**

One Saturday Steve set out. He loaded up his dad's lawnmower, some garden tools and trash bags. He found the worst-looking home in the neighborhood and walked up to the door totally unannounced.

Knock, knock.

Steve waited for well over three minutes.

Knock, knock.

Just as he decided to leave, a face appeared at the screen door.

"Yep?"

"Hi ma'am. My name's Steve and I go to the church there on the corner."

"Yep."

"Well, you see, I was just noticing your house here. And I was curious if I could help you clean things up a bit."

"What's wrong with my lawn, boy? You have a problem with my lawn?"

"Well, no. I just thought that I could help you maybe pick up some of this stuff that's in your yard. Maybe make it look a little better."

The lady began yelling at Steve. It seemed that she liked the things that were in her yard. And she let Steve know that the last thing she needed was someone from the other side of town coming to her house and telling her how she needed to keep up her lawn.

Steve left the house, went home and decided that he'd never help anyone again.

After you've read the story, discuss:

Did Steve do anything wrong? He needed to be more tactful. Perhaps he needed to pray and have others pray for him. It might be safer to work in a group.

What might have been a better way for Steve to serve the people in the neighborhood? He might have gone door to door and asked if anyone needed some yard work done—for free—rather than tell someone her yard was a mess!

Should we only attempt to serve people who are like us? Why? No, because we need to show the love of Jesus to everyone.

When we hit a difficult spot in serving others, should we just quit like Steve did? Why or why not?

Explain: **Today we'll be talking about what it means to serve Jesus no matter how tough it gets.**

Option 3  Fun and Games

You'll need Five Ping-Pong balls, a large sheet of paper, felt-tip pens, masking tape and a bag of candy.

Ahead of time, draw a huge bull's-eye of four concentric circles on the large sheet of paper. Label the outside circle "easy work," the next circle "medium work," the third circle "hard work" and the inside circle "mega-hard work." Tape the paper on the wall at the front of the meeting room. Wrap Ping-Pong balls with the masking tape with the sticky side out.

Greet students warmly; then ask for five volunteers. Explain that you're going to ask the volunteers to toss one of the Ping-Pong balls at the bull's-eye. When the ball lands in one of the circles, the audience must choose the corresponding task for the student who threw the ball. For example, if a ball lands in the "medium work" area, the audience might suggest a job like combing the hair of someone in the audience. Or if a ball lands in the "hard work" area, the audience might suggest rearranging the room. **Note:** Make sure that students suggest tasks that are appropriate both in terms of level of difficulty and in terms of how much time you have.

Once a volunteer has received an assignment, have him or her stand aside and wait for the other volunteers to complete their toss. When every volunteer has tossed a ball and received an assignment, explain that they must work fast to complete their assignments. Give them the signal to begin. As volunteers are working, encourage the rest

of the class to cheer them on. Reward the volunteers with the candy.

When students are finished, congratulate them on their efforts; then discuss:

How does having different responsibilities feel?

Were your jobs fair?

What's the difference between easy service and hard service?

Is everyone called to do the same type of service? Explain your answer.

Why should we help others?

Transition to the next step by explaining: **Today we'll be discussing** *why* **we should serve as well as** *how* **we should do it.**

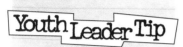

STEP 2 — MOVING UP

This step helps students realize that serving others is like serving Jesus.

Option 1 — Move It

You'll need Several Bibles, a long table, six rolls of toilet paper, a bucket of water, six plastic or paper cups and six pieces of cardboard (or paper plates).

Ahead of time, write out the following sets of Scripture passages from Matthew 25, each on a separate piece of paper: 31-34; 35,36; 37,38; 39,40; 41-43; 44-46.

Have students get into six groups and assign each group one of the Scripture passage sets. Give each group a piece of cardboard (or paper plate), a roll of toilet paper and a plastic or paper cup. Have them fill the cup with water from the bucket.

Explain that each group is to read the passage that they've been assigned; then brainstorm ways they could make that passage into a sculpture using the toilet paper and water.

When the groups are finished, display their creations in scriptural order on the table at the front of the room. Once the sculptures are arranged in order, begin reading the passage. When you come to the end of an assigned section, have the group for that section present their sculpture.

When the groups have finished reading their sections and presenting their sculptures, ask:

Who is the Son of Man? Jesus.

What does "he will separate the sheep from the goats" mean? It means that He will judge us.

Why are the sheep allowed to enter heaven and the goats aren't? Because the sheep did what Jesus asked.

Who do the righteous represent? People who *do* what God asked.

Who does the king represent? God.

Why did Jesus tell His disciples this parable? He wants them to understand the importance He places on serving the people society has forgotten.

Help students realize that the disciples wanted to have the title of "disciple," but preferred not to work hard for it. Jesus wants part of our job description to read "take care of people that others have forgotten."

How is it possible to serve people the way Jesus wants us to? We need to rely on God's power.

If you ask Jesus to take over your life but then don't serve, will you still go to heaven? Yes, you will go to heaven, but you won't experience the true joy of following and serving Him here on earth.

Explain: **Jesus wants us to see that when we serve people who are in need or destitute we are really serving Him. It's important that we adopt this attitude in our lives. We can't just serve people one day a year and think that's enough. Jesus wants us to make serving Him by serving others a key part of our lives as His followers.**

Discuss:

How are we supposed to make this part of our lives?

How easy is it to do what Jesus says?

Can everyone serve in the way Jesus is asking?

Explain to students that next you're going to explore how to make serving a reality in our lives.

Option 2 — Chat Room

You'll need Several Bibles, paper and pens or pencils.

Distribute the paper and pens or pencils and explain: **As we dive into the passage today I want you to think about what the job description might be for a Christian. Think about it—every job you'll have in life will have some sort of description, so I'd like you to imagine what a Christian's job description would be. Find a partner and together write a job description for a Christian.** When pairs are finished, have them share their descriptions with the rest of the class; then discuss:

What things did you leave off your descriptions that others included?

Did any of you put "serving others" on your descriptions?

How important is serving others to our lives as believers?

Explain: **I'd like you to read a passage where Jesus tells us that part of our job descriptions is to serve others.** Distribute Bibles and have students open to Matthew 25:31-46. Ask them to follow along with you as you read. When you're finished reading, discuss:

Who is the Son of Man? Jesus.

Who are the sheep? People who serve the needy.

Who are the goats? People who don't serve.

What does "he will separate the sheep from the goats" mean? It means that He will judge us.

Why are the sheep allowed to enter heaven and the goats aren't? Because the sheep did what Jesus asked.

Who do the righteous represent? People who *do* what God asked—those who follow Jesus.

Who does the king represent? God.

Bible Bonus Note

A good axiom when studying Scripture is never to make a doctrine out of a single verse or passage. Someone who reads only Matthew 25:31-46 and doesn't read a single other Bible verse might conclude that serving others is what gets you into heaven. We know from John 3:16, Ephesians 2:8,9 and 1 John 1:12 that the one and only thing that gets you into heaven is receiving the gift of salvation through Jesus Christ. Jesus' parable in Matthew 25 makes a dramatic point about serving, but it shouldn't be the only text we study to discover the path of salvation.

Why did Jesus tell His disciples this parable? He wanted them to understand the importance that He places on serving the people that society has forgotten.

Help students realize that the disciples wanted to have the title of "disciple," but preferred not to work hard for it. Jesus has told us that a Christian's job description is to "take care of people that others have forgotten."

Option 3 — Pulse Points

You'll need Several Bibles, candy or some other kind of food reward, one 3x5-inch index card for each student and masking tape.

Ahead of time, divide the index cards in half and write the words "Server" and "Servee" on an equal number of cards.

The Big Idea

Jesus wants us to serve others.

The Big Question

What does it mean to serve others?

Read Matthew 25:31-46 aloud; then explain: **This passage is often used to describe how Jesus will judge people when He returns to earth, but there are also three incredible truths here about what it means to serve others.**

1. Serving others means we respond to people's needs.

Explain: **In this passage, the righteous people responded to specific needs, such as the thirst and hunger of people who didn't have water or food.**

Distribute the "Server" and "Servee" index cards evenly and instruct students to find someone with the opposite kind of card. The "Servee" should let the "Server" know one need that he or she could meet right then and there, such as walking him over to the drinking fountain, helping him find a seat closer to the front of your room, or giving her a quick shoulder rub. Give students a few minutes to respond to each other's specific needs.

2. Serving others means we serve Jesus.

Explain: **Jesus makes it pretty clear that serving others is like serving Jesus. We might not see Him physically, but we know that He is pleased with what we are doing.**

Now have students switch rolls so that the "Server" becomes the "Servee." Give "Servers" a few minutes to meet the need of the "Servee"; then ask students to imagine that Jesus is watching them and is pleased with what they are doing. If you have time, ask students to share how it felt to serve someone, knowing that Jesus was pleased with what they are doing, as if He were the actual recipient of the service.

3. Serving others means we receive rewards.

Explain: **In Matthew 25:46 we see a great reward for serving: entrance into God's kingdom and eternal life. Now we know from lots of other passages in Scripture (see John 3:16; John 14:6; 1 John 1:12) that it's God's grace and our faith in Christ that saves us, so this verse needs to be interpreted within the context of the rest of the Bible, but it sure does show the importance of serving and that we will be rewarded when we serve others.**

Depending on the size of the group, give each student who has served some kind of reward, ranging from a piece of candy to a gift certificate to the local ice cream store. With junior highers, food can be a tangible teaching tool!

NOTES

STEP 3

MOVING ON

This step shows students how they can serve in the way Jesus asks them to.

Option 1 Chat Room

You'll need One paper cup of water for each student.

Before you begin the discussion, make sure that each student has a cup of water. It might be easier for you to give each student an empty cup and begin this step at a water fountain (or have pitchers of cold water available).

Instruct students not to drink the water. Explain: **We're all going to go for a short walk. When Jesus asks us to help people it's like giving us a cup of water and saying, "Someone is thirsty; go find that person and give him or her something to drink."** Follow me to find some thirsty people.

Lead students to your church's sanctuary (If a service is in progress, don't go in!) and ask:

What types of thirsty people might be here?

Are these the types of people Jesus might want us to help?

How might we help these people?

Stop next at the front door of your church. Explain to students that people come to church for a variety of reasons. Ask:

Why do people come to this church?

Are these the types of people Jesus wants us to help?

How might we help these people?

Lead students outside to a sidewalk. Ask:

What types of people pass our church every day?

Are these the people Jesus wants us to help?

How might we help them?

Lead students back to the meeting room. Ask:

Who passes through this room?

Which of your friends is Jesus calling you to help?

How might you help them?

Ask students to look at their cups of water. Explain:

Your cup of water represents spiritual and physical help. I'd like you to think about people you have contact with who might need these things. It might be someone you notice on the street or it might be someone you know very well. Either way—Jesus calls us to serve. **Who do you need to serve?** Read Matthew 10:40-42 and discuss what this passage is saying about serving others. Have students trade their cups of water with another person in the group and drink the water.

Option 2  Real Life

You'll need A female friend to help you.

Ahead of time, arrange for your friend to rush into the room and interrupt the class, saying, "Hey, I'm sorry to bug you but I've got a bunch of boxes to unload and I don't know what to do. Can you please come help me?"

Begin to repeat the point of Step 2 as your friend comes in and interrupts class. Make sure you clearly tell your friend that you can't help right now. See how the students respond as you keep talking about the importance of service. After the exchange, debrief students by discussing: **Do you think I should have helped that woman? Why? Did any of you want to get up and help even though I said we were busy?** If any students did try to go help, affirm those students for their servant attitude.

Read James 2:14-16. Explain: **God is calling us to serve others all the time. What He's looking for is an attitude of service. He wants us to be mindful of people who need to be served. If we can learn to notice people who are needy, we'll not just notice the need, we'll also be able to do more than just give lip service to a need—we'll actually do something to meet it.**

Option 3  Tough Questions

You'll need Nothing except these questions.

1. **Why does Jesus make such a big deal out of serving others?** Jesus makes a big deal about it because He knows that it's easy to forget about poor, needy and helpless people. He also wants us to focus more on others and not so much on ourselves.

2. **How can we serve people the way God asks, and still carry on with our lives?** God asks us to serve whenever we see a need. So in one sense we can't have a clear separation between the two. The most important thing is to do as much as we believe God is calling us to do, which is probably more than we are doing now.

3. **What are the earthly rewards to serving people?** We can feel good knowing that we've helped someone in need or that someone might want to know more about Christ because of our service. There is no greater reward than seeing someone come to know Christ because that person saw His love in your service.

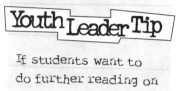

If students want to do further reading on this topic, introduce them to the book *Rock Your World* by Susie Shellenberger (Ann Arbor, MI: Vine Books, 1998). This book gives them great ideas for serving where they are. Also, *Fresh Ideas 6: Missions and Service Projects* (Jim Burns, gen. ed. and Mike DeVries; Gospel Light, 1999) is another good resource for learning to serve others.

NOTES

STEP  MOVING OUT

This step asks students to choose one specific way they can serve others this week.

 ## Option 1 — Light the Fire

You'll need Your Bible, a broom and a piece of notebook paper.

Explain: **Jesus has called us to serve Him by serving others. What an awesome opportunity—we get to serve the Creator of the universe! He wants us to be on the lookout for people and places to serve. I'd like you to look at your life. Every day you pass people who need God's touch.** Hold up the broom and explain that it represents chances we have to serve our family at home. Pass it around the room, asking students to share one way they can serve their families this week. Next hold up the piece of paper, explaining that it represents all the opportunities we have to serve our friends and teachers at school. Pass the paper around the room, asking students to share one way they can serve their school friends or teachers this week. (**Note:** If you have more than 15 students, you might want to choose to use either the broom or the paper, or circulate several brooms and pieces of paper at once and ask students to share their ideas only with the student to their right.)

Read 1 Peter 4:11 and close the meeting asking God to help students love others by serving them.

 ## Option 2 — Fired Up

You'll need Your Bible.

Instruct the group to sit in a circle. As you look at each of them, explain: **I'd like you to commit to serving people. I'm going to ask you to shut your eyes and silently let God know how you feel about committing to a life of serving Him.**

After about 30 seconds, tell students to keep their eyes shut and explain that if they're ready to live a life that totally serves God, you want them to stand. If they just don't feel ready, have them stay seated. And if they aren't sure but might be willing, have them get on their knees. Let them know how proud you are of their commitments. Continue: **Serving Jesus by serving others is a call to sacrifice our lives. God calls us to give our all when we serve.** With students' eyes still closed, read 1 Peter 4:11, then close the meeting asking God to help them love others by serving them.

 ## Option 3 — Spread the Fire

You'll need Plenty of time to do this step and an adult volunteer for every 6 to 10 students.

Ahead of time, brainstorm with the adult volunteers to come up with some service ideas to use as suggestions if needed during this step.

Have students form groups of 6 to 10, making sure that students who don't know many others join a group (or maybe form their own group). Explain: **We can use service as a way to help our friends see the gospel in action! I'd like you to plan something that your group can do that will serve someone else. Whatever you plan, make it something that your unchurched friends can help with too, so they can see that Christians do more than just sit around—they act too!**

Have the adult volunteers each join a group and instruct the group to plan a service opportunity that will involve everyone in their group. Students will need to organize it and pull it off, and the adult will serve as a consultant. Your responsibility will be to find out what they have planned and when they plan to do it, as well as to offer encouragement to invite their friends to serve too. If your schedule allows, you might even want to go help them.

When the groups have finished planning, have them present their ideas. Read 1 John 3:14,15 and close the meeting with a prayer asking God to use their service as a message about following Christ.

In the next week or two, allow groups to share what they did and what the results were.

Pressure Stories

Phil and Bill want to mow lawns in their neighborhood and have difficulty finding people who will let them mow with a pair of scissors and hedge clippers.

Brenda really wanTs To serve in an orphanage in Mexico wiTh some friends from her junior high minisTry. When she arrives aT The Mexico CiTy airporT, she finds ouT There's no TranslaTor. Her Spanish is good enough To order a Taco or burriTo, buT ThaT's abouT iT.

John wants to go to the deepest part of Africa to serve the people there. But he's discouraged when his youth pastor tells him that they wouldn't be moved by his operatic rendition of Handel's "Messiah" as a witnessing tool.

Amelia is convinced that she can serve others by using her gift of painting. But she's upset to learn that the church board won't let her paint a life-size picture of Noah's Ark on the side of the church.

Devotions in Motion

WEEK SIX: SERVICE: THE SHEEP AND GOATS

DAY 1

Quick Questions

To find out what to do with your freedom, read Galatians 5:1,3,4.

God Says

If you had a whole day to do anything you wanted, what would you do?

☐ Eat pizza, watch TV and talk on the phone.

☐ Go shopping and out to the movies.

☐ Help out at a soup kitchen washing dishes.

☐ Eat sugar out of the bag with a spoon and drink chocolate syrup like water.

I Do

What would Jesus want you to do with your free day?

How is it different from what you might want to do?

How can you make your wants and Jesus' wants come together?

FOLD HERE

DAY 4

Fast Facts

Run as fast as you can to 2 Corinthians 9:1 2–15 to find out what can happen when you give with all your heart.

God Says

Maggie is great with kids so she volunteers in the nursery on Saturday nights. James is great in math so he helps tutor fourth graders. Liesel is really dependable so she makes sure all the lights are turned off in the youth group room after everyone leaves on Sundays. Max is pretty good on the drums so he plays in the worship band.

I Do

God wants us to serve Him using the talents He gave us! Everyone has some way he or she can serve his or her church and every way is important.

Pray that God will help you find a special way to serve Him and other believers today.

FasT FacTs

Hurry To Ephesians 6:7,8 and read iT carefully!

God Says

Cori was so Tired she felt sick. She hadn'T really wanTed To go To Mexico ThaT weekend buT she felt she had To. AfTer all, she ThoughT, God says I have To serve oThers.

All weekend she waiTed for The kids To say Thank you for doing a crafT wiTh her buT all They said was do more! She waiTed for The family her church group was building The house for To say Thank you, buT They didn'T say anyThing.

Cori felT cheaTed and mad—didn'T These people undersTand she had beTTer Things To do Than go To Mexico and build houses for people who didn'T care?

I Do

God never Tells you To be a servanT because really greaT Things will happen To you and The people you serve will always be graTeful. He wanTs us To serve oThers because He firsT served us.

Pray ThaT God would give you a hearT ThaT wanTs To help oTh-ers.

FOLD HERE

Quick QuesTions

Jump inTo 1 TimoThy 6:1,2 and see whaT you find!

God Says

Who are you The mosT careful To be a "good ChrisTian servanT" around?

☐ Your ChrisTian friends

☐ The ChrisTian family who lives down The sTreeT

☐ Your non-ChrisTian Teacher

☐ Your own family

I Do

Do you someTimes geT sloppy in living ouT your ChrisTianiTy around oTher ChrisTians?

Do you ever forgeT To serve aT church or To help your ChrisTian friends?

WhaT is one way you can serve in your church This monTh?

How to Understand the Most Popular Book in the World

On the Move

Which book is found in more homes in America than any other book?

Which book is translated into more languages than any other book?

Which book has sold more copies in Europe than any other book?

Do you have the answers to these questions? Well, it's a bit of a trick, because the answer to all three questions is the same. You guessed it...the Bible. The Bible is the most popular book in all history and is the most widely read and translated book throughout the world.

Lots of people own Bibles and have them sitting on their dressers or bookshelves. But the tragedy is that that's all they're doing—sitting there, hardly ever opened, just getting dusty.

You can't understand the Bible by letting it sit on the shelf, and even putting it under your pillow while you sleep won't work either. If you want to understand the Bible, the most popular book in the world, you have to get three things.

1. Get the Plan

Lots of times we don't read the Bible because we don't know where to start. After all, it's really big—66 books in one—written by 40 authors over a period of 1,600 years and written in three different languages: Hebrew, Greek and Aramaic. With all of that staring you in the face, how do you know where to start?

That's why you need a plan. You might choose to read just one chapter a day, or maybe even three or four chapters a day to finish the Bible in one year. You might read the books in the order they come in—starting at Genesis and ending in Revelation—or maybe read what you're learning in church. The important thing is to come up with a plan that works for YOU and lets you study the different parts of the Bible so you understand it all.

2. Get the Point

Read the text you've planned and ask yourself this important question: What does the passage mean? When people read the Bible and don't really ask that question they come up with some funky ideas. Try three things to help you figure out what a passage means. First, make sure you get a Bible that has words you can understand. There are many translations. Ask your youth leader or pastor for help. And second, make sure you read the footnotes or margin notes to help you figure out the meaning of the passage. Third, ask the Holy Spirit to help you understand what you read.

Imagine telling a friend to do something really important, and the next thing you know, he's gone off skateboarding and totally forgotten what you asked him to do. That's what happens every time we read the Bible and don't do what God says. To stop that from happening, ask yourself a second question: What does this passage mean to me? How does what it says relate to my family, friends, school, church, friends who don't know Jesus, next-door neighbors, and even the guy I talk to at the donut shop? Every time you read, come up with one specific way to apply what the Bible says to your own life.

3. GET THE TEAM

Most things in life are better and easier if you do them with someone else. The same is true with understanding the Bible. Pick one friend and ask her to be on your team and help you keep on track. Have a five-minute phone conversation with her every week to share what you're learning. Or ask her to E-mail you to see if you've read the Bible today. Just knowing that someone will ask you what Scripture you're on and what you're learning will help you to keep on track.

The bottom line: Spend a few minutes a day and make the Bible the most popular book in your life too

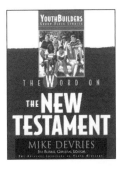
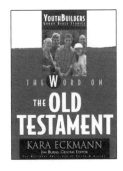
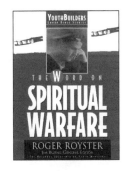